WRITING IT YOUR WAY

tell your story-
It's important!

Dan Hamer

may 2, 2018

WRITING IT YOUR WAY

A STEP-BY-STEP GUIDE TO TELLING THE STORY OF YOUR LIFE

by Ann Hamer

ISBN: 0692784950
ISBN 13: 9780692784952

To
Mom
You're the best
and
My brother Rick
For his unwavering help
when we needed it the most

ACKNOWLEDGEMENTS

First and foremost, my thanks go to my mom, Lucerne Hamer, for her unflagging love, support, and encouragement. She is truly the nicest person in the world. I love you Mom.

Secondly, to the members of our autobiography classes and other contributors who have so willingly shared their stories and their friendship. You have all taught me so much: Jeanne Behr, M.B., Lynda Barr, C.H.B., Dean and Denise B., Pola B., Barbara Cauthorn, Maria C., Joanne C., Susan Fraizer, Alexandra and Raul Gutierrez, Crissie Jeston, Joy Karsevar, Luna, Jeanne Master, G.O., Aurora Reinhart, Sallie Ringle, Mel Sever, Bill Shearer, Jan S., Rosemary Ventura, and Joan Wallach.

Thanks also to the City of Upland, California and Gibson Senior Center for giving our autobiography classes a home.

And finally, a heartfelt thanks goes to the people who read my manuscript and offered their suggestions and feedback: Priscilla Fernandez, Rick Hamer, Crissie Jeston, Marsha Price, and Joan Wallach. Dear friends and careful readers - and there is nothing better than that.

TABLE OF CONTENTS

FOREWORD

My mother and I were talking about my father shortly after his death in March of 2013. Although she was married to him for 64 years, and I lived with him for the first 18 years of my life, we both felt that we knew so very little about him. He had taken a writing class after he retired, so we had his stories of growing up in Michigan, his military service, his career, and his life after he married and had children. But, about who this man was - what he thought and felt, what motivated him, what were his dreams, disappointments, hopes, fears, and accomplishments, the things in which he took the most pride, and the things he most regretted - we knew nothing. My father was a very private man. He revealed very little about himself, and now the chance to truly know him was gone. After we realized this, Mom and I decided to create a class in guided autobiography to help others tell their life stories.

We think old age will never come. Somehow we'll outlive the fate of all the generations that came before us and never grow old, never get infirm or forgetful, and never die. But life happens, and years pass and then more years pass, and then it's too late. So tell your story. Tell it now and record your place in time.

You and your life story are important and matter to us all, not just to your family and friends. You are a part of history. There are things you experienced as a child that are totally foreign to generations brought up with the internet and computers, but without the Cold War and nuclear arms race. Remember drop drills, mimeograph machines, "Wite-Out", and the miracle of correcting Selectric typewriters? Remember dress codes in school and job postings in newspapers listed under "Help Wanted - Male" and "Help Wanted - Female"? I remember all these things, and believe me, I don't feel old at all!

You may think you don't need to tell your story. You may feel that when you compare yourself to others, you are not as educated, or as well traveled, or as successful, or as attractive, and so you are reluctant to write your story. Whether or not you have family and friends with whom to share, the story of you and your life is important. It is part of the fabric of society; it is the history of your town, your country, and your world. If you were a historian, just think how excited you would be to discover the diary of a "real" person living a "normal" life, rather than yet another biography of a general, a politician, a ruler, or the wealthy. Most of us are not presidents or movie stars. We are the "regular people" who make the engine of society work, and our stories truly do matter. Your successes inspire, and your failures provide lessons and warnings.

ONE

Welcome to the journey that is your life. As you begin this journey, you may feel overwhelmed. There are just too many memories, too much to write, and not enough time. Writing your autobiography may feel like you're in the Himalayan foothills, staring at the insurmountable obstacle of Mt. Everest, thinking, "I'm going to climb *that*?" Yes you are. Just as you would climb Everest one step at a time and with the help of others, you will use this guide to help you write the story of your life, taking it one step at a time.

There is a lot in this book. There are over 400 writing prompts, and many of the prompts incorporate questions and suggestions to help you tell your story. As you look through this book, it may seem just too hard. After all, you're not in school and you probably don't want to write another paper *ever again*!

Go through this guide and select a few things to write about. Jot down a few notes. There are no deadlines, so take your time. When you go to a restaurant you don't order everything on the menu. Treat this book as the menu for telling your life story. Select a tasty appetizer here, a substantial entrée there, and the dessert of a sweet memory.

And then dig in. It's time for you to write the story of your life.

HELPFUL HINT #1 - GETTING STARTED

Make a commitment to yourself to write every day. Even if you manage only a few words, at least once a day take up your pen or sit at your computer and write.

Begin by looking through all the exercises in this book. Select a few topics that catch your attention and bring some memories to mind that encourage you to start writing. And then begin.

As you work through the exercises in this book, remember that you do not need to answer every question or respond to every exercise. If a question helps you get started or brings to mind thoughts and memories, then answer it. If a question doesn't seem to apply to you, skip it or come back to it later when it does apply.

The important thing is to start writing!!

#1 - EARLY

<u>What is your earliest memory?</u>

Your notes:_____

_____

_____

_____

#2 - NEIGHBORHOOD

Visualize the first place where you lived and the first neighborhood you remember from your childhood.

<u>What did it look like?</u>
- Urban
- Rural
- Suburban

<u>What features do you remember?</u>
- Your home
- Human-made and natural features
- Neighbors
- Structures
- Geographical features
- Rivers, lakes, ocean
- Scary places
- Where the treasure was buried
- Your favorite hiding place
- Schools
- Stores

<u>Illustrate your visualization by drawing either a map or a picture</u>

Your notes:_____

_____

_____

_____

#3 - WHO ARE YOU?

<u>What is your full name?</u>
<u>Is there a story behind your name?</u>
- Were you named after someone – family member, family friend, famous person?
- Was your name popular when you were born?
- Did many children in your neighborhood or school had the same name?

<u>Does your name truly describe *you*?</u>
- If your name doesn't seem to fit, and you could choose another, what would it be?
- Why would this name fit you better than the name you have?

Your notes:_____

_____

_____

_____

❧

"The Origin of My Name"
by Alexandra Gutierrez

The day I learned the origin of my real name I was taken aback. My mom told me that my real name is Alejandra. I was named after two of my aunts.

The first aunt was only six when she passed. My grandmother Manula had left her in the care of a relative while she went off to look for work. When she found work in the laundry of the next town, she sent for her daughter. The relative boarded herself and the daughter onto a push-pull cart on the railroad track. As they began their jaunt, a train collided with the cart, and both tragically perished.

At age 19, the second aunt also met with tragedy. She was a young and beautiful girl - full of life and a gifted pianist. Unfortunately, she lived in an era when the pregnancy of an unwed daughter was cause for disgrace. Her parents (my grandparents) met the news with anger and despair. They argued inces-santly about how to handle the problem. Should they send her away? Cover-up the pregnancy by having my grandmother wear a pillow under her dress? Or deal with the stigma of having an unwed daughter?

Rather than embrace their daughter's pain, they berated her, and in no uncertain terms let her know what a disappointment she was. In despair, and in the heat of the moment, my aunt picked up a gun, ran down the hill, and shot herself to death.

This aunt, Alejandrina, had taken on the role of nanny to my mom because my grandmother worked all the time while my mother was growing up. When I came along, my mom wanted to name me af-ter her beloved sister Alejandrina, but my grandmother protested vehemently. She argued that she had already lost two daughters with that name. She didn't want to tempt fate with another calamity. After much deliberation, they settled on a compromise, and named me Alejandra, a derivative of Alejandrina.

I like to ponder on how my name came to be. I like to think of how my mom spoke of my aunt with admira-tion and love, and how she wanted to pass that affection on to me. I like the sound of my name. I think of it as regal. Unfortunately, no one calls me by my real name Alejandra.

Most people call me Sandy. Again, another derivative. Think Alexandra, Andra, Sandra, Sandy. My im-mediate family calls me Sandra, my friends call me Sandy, my nieces and nephews call me Aunt Dot, and before I was married, my siblings called me Sister. Who knows???

#4 - NICKNAME

<u>Do you have a nickname?</u>
- How did you get it?

<u>Are you commonly known by your nickname, or is it used only by your family and friends?</u>
- Did you have a nickname as a child that you no longer use?
- Do you have a different nickname now?

<u>Did you have a different name at home than you had at school?</u>

Your notes:_____

_____

_____

_____

#5 - GROWING UP - YOUR CHILDHOOD

<u>When and where were you born?</u>
<u>Who were the members of your family?</u>
- Father, Mother, siblings
- Other relatives who lived with you
- Non-related household members
- Foster parents

<u>Who were you in the family?</u>
- Oldest child – leader of the pack
- Youngest child – baby
- Only child
- Peacemaker
- Brat
- Troublemaker
- Mother's helper
- Dad's little man
- Princess
- Daddy's girl
- Tomboy
- Or?

<u>What was the role of other family members?</u>
- Breadwinner
- Stay-at-home parent
- Bossy older sibling
- Protective brother or sister
- Or?

<u>What activities did your family regularly do together?</u>
- Eat meals
- Vacation
- Work in a family business
- Attend worship services
- Share bedtime stories
- And?

<u>Were you close to your extended family, i.e. grandparents, aunts, uncles, cousins?</u>

Your notes:_____

_____

_____

_____

HELPFUL HINT #2 - STATE YOUR OBJECTIVES

Create a list of your objectives. When you are stuck, refer to your list to regain your focus and remember why you are writing your story.

Start by writing, "I am doing this because … " Remember, any reasons you have for writing your autobiography are valid, because this is your story and they are your reasons. There are no right or wrong answers.

Here are some suggestions. You may have others.
- I want to leave a written legacy for my family and friends
- I want my family to know about my life
- I want people to remember me
- I have important things to say and I want to share my wisdom

- I want to help people avoid making the same mistakes I made
- I want to explain my actions
- I am misunderstood and want people to know who I really am
- Lots of interesting things happened to me
- I want to re-live my past
- I'm an interesting person
- I'm a nice person

#6 - CHILDHOOD HOME

<u>What was your childhood residence?</u>
- House, apartment, farm
- Orphanage, group home, foster home

<u>What was the community like?</u>
- Urban, rural, suburban
- Desert, beach, mountains, plains
- Special landmarks

<u>Weather</u>
- Four seasons
- Temperate
- Tropical or subtropical

<u>Write as many specific details of your childhood home as you can</u>
- Rooms
- Furnishings and décor
- Yard
- Garage or car port
- Attic
- Cellar
- Favorite hiding place

What was your favorite room in the house?

What was stored in the attic, cellar, and garage?

Did you live in the same home while growing up or move around a lot?

- If you moved around a lot, why?

Your notes:_____

_____

_____

_____

#7 - SLEEPING

Do you stay up late or go to bed early?

- Are you an early riser or a late riser?

Have your sleeping habits changed as you've aged?

Your notes:_____

_____

_____

_____

#8 - RUN AWAY

Did you ever run away from home?

- How old were you when you first ran away?
- What made you decide to run away the first time?
- Did you run away more than once?

What happened to you when you returned home?

Your notes:_____

_____

_____

_____

#9 - POCKET MONEY

<u>Did you get an allowance when you were growing up?</u>
- What chores did you do to earn your allowance?

<u>Did you have an after school or part-time job?</u>
- What was the job?
- What did you like about this job?
- What did you dislike about this job?

<u>Did you get cash gifts from family and friends?</u>

Your notes:_____

_____

_____

_____

#10 - FAMILY RESEMBLANCE

<u>How are you similar to your parents and siblings?</u>
- Who in your family are you most like?

<u>How are you different from your parents and siblings?</u>
- Who in your family are you least like?

Your notes:_____

_____

_____

_____

TWO

HELPFUL HINT #3 - WRITE A MISSION STATEMENT

Writing a mission statement or first chapter may help you focus and decide what you are trying to accomplish. You may want to use your life story as the basis for a novel, turn your journals into something you can share with your family, or preserve your stories for future generations.

Begin with a mission statement or first chapter <u>only</u> if it helps you start writing. If instead of helping, it freezes you or makes your task seem too gigantic to even begin, don't do it! Find some other way to get started, even if it means that you start small.

#11 - YOUR PARENTS (1)

<u>Did you grow up with one parent or two?</u>
<u>Was the parental role assumed by someone other than your biological father or mother?</u>
- Step parents
- Foster parents
- Adoptive parents
- Siblings
- Other family members or family friends
- Group home or orphanage

Your notes:_____

_____

_____

_____

#12 - YOUR PARENTS (2)

<u>What did your parents do for employment?</u>
- Did both parents work outside the home?
- Did you have a stay-at-home parent?

Your notes:_____

_____

_____

_____

#13 - YOUR PARENTS (3)

<u>What activities did you do with your parents?</u>
- Parents who were Scout leaders
- Parents who coached sporting teams
- Parents who transported you to lessons and after school activities
- Or?

Your notes:_____

_____

_____

_____

"My Family"
by Lucerne Hamer

My mother and father married young. She was seventeen and he was twenty. They both liked to dance and met and then dated at the ballrooms which were popular in those days. They were married September 26, 1923. They were loving parents, and my brother Frank and I were so very fortunate to be their children. My father worked at his father's business, Sasine & Son Machine Tool and Die Works in Los Angeles. Making movie splicers for Eastman Kodak carried the business through the Depression. During World War II, they made machined aircraft parts for Douglas and North American.

I loved to watch my father's mother, Grandma Sasine, make strudel. She would cover the kitchen table with a cloth, and then roll and roll the dough until it was stretched paper thin over the table. I have never eaten strudel to compare with my Grandma's. Grandma and Grandpa S. would also take me to the Turner Club. The adults played cards, ate and talked, almost entirely in German. During World War II Turner Clubs were closed. They were considered subversive.

Thanksgiving was at my other Grandma's with turkey and all the fixings. We were a small family so it was Frank and me, our parents, our grandparents and our Auntie Ann, my father's sister. Christmas dinner was at the Sasine grandparents. Grandma S. made cookies that were supposedly a favorite of Emperor Franz Joseph. I was told she had been a cook in one of his palaces, and that was how she had the recipe. I have the recipe and often make the cookies at Christmas. They are a bit tricky and one recipe makes 44 dozen cookies.

In 1938 my mother's mother, Grandma Kennedy, bought a lot for my parents in Hermosa Beach. They built a house on the 30x90 foot lot on 17th Street. Except for the time I was at USC, I lived there until I married in 1949. It was a great street. There were children of our ages. We played hide and seek, kick the can, and hit the bat. We were enrolled in swim lessons at the Surf and Sand Club, later the Hermosa Biltmore, now demolished and replaced by condos. It was a salt water pool and even to this day I cannot get used to a fresh water pool. We became good swimmers. When older, we could go to the beach without a parent, but were never allowed to swim alone. We especially liked to swim in the late afternoon when the waves were larger. I was never very good at catching waves, but it was exciting when I did. Frank surfed with a long hollow wooden paddle board, which he had to stand on its end to drain after use. I never tried to ride his board because it was way too big for me. Frank was 6'4".

We went to the movies at the local theater a few blocks from home. Our parents liked to sit in the more expensive loge seats because they were more comfortable and had better viewing. There was a double feature, newsreel, cartoon and sometimes an extra short film. You could come in at any time. After the movie we would walk to the drugstore soda fountain. Father's favorite was a pineapple soda. Of course there were the Saturday kid matinees with the exciting serial and appropriate double feature. Seats were 10 cents and Frank and I got extra money to purchase candy at the store next to the theater. There was no snack bar in the theater.

One summer Mother, Frank, and I went to Pinecrest Resort, near Lake Arrowhead. Father had to work, so he came up weekends during the month we were there. After breakfast I headed for the barn and spent nearly all day riding, grooming, and being around horses. In the evening there were programs, music, dancing, and games in the resort's lounge. It was a fun place and great for families. It was closed by the time I wanted to take my three children there many years later.

#14 - YOUR PARENTS (4)

<u>Was there anything your parents were especially strict about?</u>
- Not talking to strangers
- Doing your chores
- Helping in the family business
- Honesty and keeping your word
- Doing your schoolwork
- Health and diet
- Dating
- And?

Your notes:_____

_____

_____

_____

#15 - YOUR PARENTS (5)

<u>Describe a gift you received from your father, your mother, or both your parents</u>
- A tangible gift - something special you received
- Something intangible - a skill or character trait

<u>What values did your parents give you?</u>
- Work ethic
- Religious values
- Love for family
- Loyalty
- Honesty and integrity
- And?

Your notes:_____

_____

_____

_____

#16 - YOUR PARENTS (6)

<u>Did you have a good relationship with your parents?</u>
- Did you have a better relationship with one parent than the other?

<u>What did you fight about with your parents?</u>

<u>Do you have any issues with your parents you feel are still unresolved?</u>
- What can you do to deal with these unresolved feelings?

Your notes:_____

_____

_____

_____

#17 - YOUR FATHER

How are you like your father?
- How are you unlike your father?

What did you love or admire most about your father?
- What did you dislike most about your father?

Your notes:_____

_____

_____

_____

#18 - YOUR MOTHER

How are you like your mother?
- How are you unlike your mother?

What did you love or admire most about your mother?
- What did you dislike most about your mother?

Your notes:_____

_____

_____

_____

#19 - PARENTAL ADVICE

What were the things your mother and father always said to you?
- Did you consider these to be "words of wisdom" or something to be ignored?

<u>Does your parents' advice seem much wiser now than when you were a child?</u>
- Do you find yourself repeating to your children or grandchildren things your parents said to you?

<u>What were the things your parents said to you that you swore you'd **never** say to your own children?</u>

Your notes:_____

_____

_____

_____

#20 - READING (1)

<u>What books did you read and love as a child and pre-teen?</u>
- Do you still re-read any of these books as an adult?

Your notes:_____

_____

_____

_____

#21 - READING (2)

<u>Is reading for pleasure something you just don't do?</u>
- Why?

<u>Were there any issues that made reading difficult for you, i.e. dyslexia?</u>
- Were your learning difficulties ever diagnosed and treated?
- If they went undiagnosed when you were a child, how long was it before you were diagnosed and treated?

Your notes:_____

_____

_____

_____

══

HELPFUL HINT #4 - BE READY TO WRITE DAY AND NIGHT

Keep a pen and piece of paper near your bed or in the TV room so you can jot down thoughts and memories as they occur to you. When you go for a walk take along pen and paper or a hand-held recording device. It's easy to tell yourself you will remember something, and just as easy to forget. By keeping pen and paper handy, you will be able to make a note of things as the books you read or the shows you watch or the things you see waken your memories and remind you of past events in your life.

══

#22 - CAKE

Celebrations often involve cake. Think of weddings and birthdays, a cake traditional in your family for holidays and special occasions, or the cake you entered in a competition.

<u>Write about your favorite cake</u>
<u>Here are some suggestions</u>
- The first cake you baked by yourself
- A special cake you baked with your mother or grandmother
- The best cake you ever made
- The best cake you ever tasted

- A prize-winning cake
- The cake you always have for special occasions
- The cake you had for a special celebration, i.e. a wedding cake
- A cake you had on a special vacation or trip
- A cake that just didn't turn out right

Your notes:_____

_____

_____

_____

#23 - ARE YOU

Are you country or rock and roll?
A race car or a sedan?
A dog or a cat?
- Why?

Your notes:_____

_____

_____

_____

#24 - GAMES KIDS PLAY

What games did you play when you were growing up?
- Kick the can
- Hide and seek
- Sandbox
- Computer games
- Horses

- Dungeons and Dragons
- House
- Board games and card games
- Cowboys and the "Wild West"
- Combat and war
- Holiday games
- Dodgeball, "four square", tetherball
- Games based on TV shows or movies
- Astronaut or space explorer
- Spy
- Magician or wizard
- And?

What games did you play as a child that you'd like to play again?
- Will you?

Your notes:_____

_____

_____

_____

#25 - TOYS

What were your favorite toys as a child?
- Crayons, paint, and clay
- Slinky, Silly Putty, Hula Hoop
- Puzzles
- Cap pistols and BB guns
- Toy soldiers
- Scooters and bikes
- Ice skates and roller skates
- Sleds
- Model building kits

- Electric trains
- Matchbox cars
- Tinker Toys and Erector Sets
- Legos and Lincoln Logs
- Microscopes and chemistry sets
- Animal figurines and models
- Stuffed, plush, and soft toys
- Mini kitchen appliances
- Dolls
- And?

Your notes:_____

_____

_____

_____

#26 - MISCONCEPTIONS

What misconceptions did you have as a child?
- Were they due to misinformation, i.e. where babies came from
- Were they due to something you misheard, i.e. "Olive the other reindeer" instead of "All of the other reindeer"

When did you discover the truth?
- How did you feel when you discovered the truth?

Your notes:_____

_____

_____

_____

#27 - FAMILY STORIES AND LEGENDS

<u>What are the family stories and legends you want to tell that may be lost forever if you do not preserve them now?</u>
- What stories did your parents, grandparents and great-grandparents tell you about their lives?

<u>Do you have any family heirlooms?</u>
- What are the family stories that go with these heirlooms?
- Do you have any photos showing members of your family using these heirlooms?

Your notes:_____

_____

_____

_____

#28 - YOUR GRANDPARENTS

<u>What is the story of your grandparents?</u>
- Names
- Birth dates and birth places
- The stories your grandparents told you about their youth and young adulthood
- How your grandparents met and married
- If they are deceased, when and where they died and where they are buried

Your notes:_____

_____

_____

_____

"Grandfather Santiago - The Pot of Gold in San Quentin"
by Maria C.

Santiago was my paternal grandfather. To his grandchildren he was our "Apong Ago." Ago is a short name for his full name, and Apong in Pampango (the Philippine dialect he spoke) means grandfather.

My grandfather came from a humble family. His parents must have been farmers since he grew up in Pampanga, and this region of the Philippines is known for its rice fields. I remember him saying they used to catch frogs in the rice fields and bring them home for dinner. I don't know how he met my grandmother, but I am pretty sure they grew up in the same town. I recall him saying he met my grandmother at a young age.

In his early married life my grandfather was a farmer. However, he was not content with his lot. He knew he could do better. Grandfather took a chance and ventured into the buying and selling of goods. He became a Viajero. The word Viajero is a Spanish word; colloquially it means traveling salesman.

My dear Apong Ago would go by train or bus to remote towns of Pangasinan province. He supplied local markets with various dry goods such as blankets, towels, clothing, shoes, slippers, and other basic needs. He had a good head for business and knew his market. His business flourished, and he hired a crew of Viajeros to help him meet growing demand.

One of the towns Grandfather often visited was San Quentin. He saw the rice fields there were more affordable than in his own hometown. Grandfather bought several hectares of rice fields. San Quentin turned out to be his gold mine. From an ordinary farmer, my grandfather turned his life around and became a wealthy landowner, well beyond his imagination.

Through this vast property, he was able to support his family in a lifestyle he had not enjoyed. Apong Ago's hard work and investments paid off. My grandfather paid for my dad's medical school and then sent him to post-graduate studies at Columbia University in New York. During those days, only the old rich and established families could send their children to study abroad. There were no scholarships or government assistance. Indeed, my grandfather "leap-frogged" to a new social status.

When I was in high school, grandfather suffered a stroke. He was paralyzed and had slurred speech. After his stroke he completely withdrew from the world. Most of the time Apong Ago had a blank stare, and didn't talk much. Certainly a far cry from the tough, confident, intense grandfather I knew growing up.

One summer evening in May, 1974, my sisters, Josie, Cita, cousins, Alice and Lettie, and I decided to visit our grandfather. We were just back from a bridal shower, and it seemed like a good time to drop by. After all, we hadn't seen him for a while. When we got there, his caregiver was spoon feeding him a bowl of chicken rice soup. It was pitiful to see Grandfather in that state. In his younger years, Apong Ago was known for his huge appetite. His table spread would be a five course meal, with soup, entrees of his favorite beef, pork, chicken, fish, and finally a rich dessert. Now, my poor grandfather could not even finish a bowl of bland soup.

We circled around, cheering him on to finish his soup. Even with our positive vibes and enthusiasm, there was no reaction from my grandfather. It was just his normal blank stare. Since this was a depressing scene for us, we decided not to stay long. Our grandfather didn't say a word, but we all noticed tears rolling down his cheeks. He looked extremely sorrowful, and he was peering intently at each one of us. We thought nothing much of this incident when we left the house.

The moment my sisters and I got back to our parents' house, my mother got a call. My grandfather had passed away. We thought this was not possible since we had seen him less than an hour before. Our beloved grandfather died while we were on our way home. He must have sensed death was coming, and cried because he was leaving us. Apong Ago died that fateful evening of May 15, 1974.

Grandfather Santiago gave us a bright future. Our family and the present generation would not be where we are now if not for his vision, hard work, and the tremendous sacrifices he made in his early years. Apong Ago's investments and good fortune all trickled down to our generation.

Thank you, dear grandfather Santiago, your life story is indeed an inspiration to all of us, and rightfully deserves to be told to your great-grandchildren and great-great-grandchildren.

I love you my dear grandfather, Apong Ago!

#29 - BLACK SHEEP

<u>Who are the infamous or villainous members of your family?</u>
- What actions earned these family members their reputation?

<u>Do you know their side of the story?</u>

Your notes:_____

_____

_____

_____

#30 - FAMILY MYSTERIES

<u>What are the unresolved mysteries in your family?</u>
- A mysterious disappearance
- An unexplained death
- The reason for a suicide
- Or?

<u>What do family members believe are the explanations for these mysteries?</u>
- What do you believe?

Your notes:_____

_____

_____

_____

#31 - COMING TO AMERICA

<u>How and why did your family come to the US?</u>
- Where were your parents, grandparents and great-grandparents born?
- If they were born outside the US, why did they immigrate?
- How did you and your family end up living where you live now?
- Was your family name changed in any way to make it more "Western" or easier to pronounce?

<u>If you were the only one who immigrated to the US, why did the rest of your family choose to stay in the "old country"?</u>
- Why did you choose to immigrate?

<u>If your parents or other family members did not immigrate to the US or settle near you:</u>
- How often do you see them?
- Where do you meet?
- How do you stay in touch?
- What family events and milestones did you miss due to separation and distance?

Your notes:_____

_____

_____

_____

#32 - ODDEST

<u>Describe your oddest or most eccentric relative</u>

Your notes:_____

_____

_____

_____

THREE

- Gather together photos, diaries, journals, scrapbooks, school yearbooks, and public records such as birth, marriage, and death certificates.
- Talk to family and friends, but remember your memory of an event may not be the same as theirs. Conversations may help you remember, but try not to let them color your perception of events. This is <u>your</u> story. Try to be accurate, but you don't need to be "fair". If others disagree with you, they can write their own autobiography!
- Unpack closets and boxes and take out the things you have saved. You kept those things for a reason - now is the time to tell their story.
- Play the music of your past. A song may jog your memory.
- Look through history books for photos that remind you of what you were doing at a particular time. When I look at the iconic photo of a girl kneeling by the body of a student killed by the National Guard at Kent State, I am reminded that on that day, May 4, 1970, I fell off a horse and fractured my skull. The photo of a historically significant event reminds me of a personal experience that has nothing to do with the event itself.
- If you are stuck, take a break. Go for a walk, have a snack, phone a friend. Remember this is not school, and there are no due dates or deadlines.

#33 - GOING BACK

<u>Have you ever visited the home of your ancestors?</u>
- What was that experience like?
- Did you feel any sense of "homecoming"?

Your notes:_____

_____

_____

_____

#34 - FEATHER AND FUR

<u>If you could be any animal, what animal would you be?</u>
- Would you choose to be a wild animal, a domesticated animal, a bird, a reptile, or your own well-loved pet?

<u>What characteristics of this animal do you want to have?</u>
- How would you act if you were this animal?

Your notes:_____

_____

_____

_____

#35 - ACTING UP

<u>Were you often in trouble as a child?</u>
<u>How were you punished when you misbehaved?</u>
- Were these punishments fair?

<u>Did you get in trouble at school?</u>
- What did you do that got you in trouble?

<u>What happened when you were caught?</u>
- Sent to the principal
- Detention
- Suspended or expelled
- I was never caught!

<u>What was the worst thing you did as a child and how were you punished?</u>

Your notes:_____

_____

_____

_____

#36 - SCHOOL DAYS

<u>When and where did you go to school?</u>
- Elementary school
- Middle school or junior high
- High school
- Trade school
- Public school or private school

<u>What did your school look like?</u>
- How many students were in your class and in your school?

<u>Did you walk to school, take the bus, or get taken to school by a parent or other adult?</u>
- Did you walk to school alone, with siblings, or with kids from your neighborhood?

<u>Were you a good student?</u>
- What were your favorite and least favorite subjects?

<u>What were the "fads" when you were in school?</u>
- Clothes and jewelry
- Hair styles
- Music
- TV shows and movies
- Toys and games

- Sports
- After school activities
- And?

What were your extra-curricular activities?
- Athlete or cheerleader
- School government
- School and non-school clubs
- Field trips
- Class monitor ("chalkboards", "windows", "keys")
- Drama or glee club
- And?

What did you wear?
- Was there a dress code or uniform?
- Did you get new school clothes in the fall?

What special awards or honors did you receive?
- Academic awards and scholarships
- Sports
- Good citizenship

How was your social life?
- Dating and romance
- Dances

What were your favorite school days?
- First day of school
- Holiday celebrations
- Sporting events
- Elections
- Homecoming, prom, other school dances
- A favorite class
- Special days which were part of your school's own traditions
- Last day of school before vacation

Your notes:_____

_____

_____

_____

#37 - TEACHERS

<u>Did you have a favorite teacher or counselor?</u>
- Why was this teacher or counselor special to you?

Your notes:_____

_____

_____

_____

❈

"She Made All the Difference"
by C.H.B.

I really hated high school, and in my junior year I started skipping classes. At first just a few classes here and there, but eventually I'd skip for several days in a row. Back then, if you were absent you needed a note from home, so I became proficient at forging Mom's signature. I would show up for class every once in a while, and if it happened to be a test day, I would just sit and stare. I'd write my name on top of the test paper and that would be it. It really threw my teachers for a loop. I remember one teacher saying that if I didn't take the test she'd have to flunk me. I told her to go ahead and flunk me. I just didn't care.

Mrs. Lillian Dean was my high school counselor. She kept me in school and made sure I graduated. Whenever I felt stressed or depressed, I would go talk with her. Sometimes I'd just hang out. She had over 400 students assigned to her, but she always made time for me. Her office was my refuge. Mrs.

Dean helped me graduate from high school in February, a semester early. I did not participate in the graduation ceremony in June, and did not see Mrs. Dean again after I graduated.

I have not had many people in my life who stood by me the way Mrs. Dean did. I hope I said thank you to her way back then, but I'm not sure that I did. After all, I was a teenager. I wish I had contacted her later to say how much she meant to me. Maybe I didn't say it to her then, but I'm saying it now - thank you Mrs. Dean.

#38 - AFTER SCHOOL

<u>What did you do after school?</u>
- Musical instrument, singing, or dance lessons
- Horseback riding lessons
- Soccer, football, track, gymnastics, swimming, other sports
- Boy or Girl Scouts
- Religious training
- Neighborhood play with friends
- Care for younger siblings
- Housework and meal preparation
- Work in a family business
- Or?

<u>Where did you and your friends "hang out" after school?</u>

Your notes:_____

_____

_____

_____

#39 - LANGUAGE

<u>What language was spoken in your home when you were growing up?</u>

If your parents spoke a non-English language, did you to learn to speak it?
- If not, why not?
- Did you teach your own children to speak the language of their heritage?

What languages do you speak?

Your notes:_____

_____

_____

_____

#40 - WITH

Who do you wish was with you?

Your notes:_____

_____

_____

_____

#41 - GARDEN

How does your garden grow?

Your notes:_____

_____

_____

_____

HELPFUL HINT #6 - PREPARE YOURSELF

Be prepared to write by using tools that encourage you to write.
- Pen and paper using a favorite pen and certain type of paper
- Computer
- Handwriting which you later transcribe onto your computer
- Oral dictation

Find a comfortable area to use as your "writing place".
- If you have a set place and set time to write, it may feel like going to the workplace and motivate you.
- If, on the other hand, you are happily retired and <u>love</u> not having to go to work, you may be happy taking a more relaxed approach to your writing place: in bed with your laptop, at your local coffee place, or any place at all because you always have a pen and paper on hand.

Jot down things as they come to you. Don't edit, don't even think too much, just write. In the beginning don't worry about putting your memories in chronological order. Don't worry about punctuation or spelling or grammar. Just get your thoughts down on paper. Editing and polishing can come later.

Set yourself a goal to write a certain number of pages or for a certain amount of time every day. Don't spend too much time preparing to write. It's easy to convince yourself that you're being productive when you're really just doing busy work. Keep your objectives in mind and start writing!

Remember - It isn't "writing" until you actually write it down! It doesn't count as "writing" if ideas stay in your head!!

#42 - SUMMERTIME

<u>What did you do on a typical summer's day when you were not in school?</u>
- As a child
- As a pre-teen
- As a teenager

Your notes:_____

_____

_____

_____

#43 - CAMP

<u>Did you go to camp?</u>
- Day camp or sleep-away camp
- Scouting or church camp
- Special interest camp
- Music or drama
- Weight loss
- Outward Bound
- Science
- Sports
- Cheerleading

<u>How old were you when you went to camp?</u>
- Were you homesick?

<u>Where was the camp?</u>
- Did you go to camp more than once?

<u>What activities did you do at camp?</u>
- Crafts
- Hiking
- Swimming and boating

- Horseback riding
- Campfire songs and skits
- Drama and music
- Winter sports
- Or?

Were you a camper or a counselor?

Your notes:_____

_____

_____

_____

#44 - CHILDHOOD HEALTH

What diseases, illnesses or serious accidents did you have as a child?
What impact did these illnesses and accidents have on you and your family?
- Were there any long-term effects from a childhood illness or accident that impacted the rest of your life?

Were you ever hospitalized as a child?
- What led to your hospitalization?

Your notes:_____

_____

_____

_____

#45 - STARRING

In the movie of your life, who should play you?

Your notes:_____

_____

_____

_____

#46 - COLLEGE / UNIVERSITY

<u>Did you go to college or university?</u>
- What college or university did you attend?
- Why did you choose that school?

<u>What was your major field of study?</u>
- Why did you choose that major?
- Did you go to graduate school?

<u>Did you live at home or "go away" to school?</u>
- How did you feel about leaving home?

<u>If you left home, where did you live?</u>
- Dorm
- Fraternity or sorority
- Apartment or house
- Rented a room in someone's home

<u>Were you the first in your family to go to college or university or to earn a college degree?</u>

<u>If you did not earn your degree, why did you leave college?</u>
- Did you later return to college and complete your degree?

<u>If you did not go to college or university, what did you do instead?</u>
- Work
- Marry
- Have children
- Travel
- Or?

<u>If you chose not to go to college or university, did you ever regret that decision?</u>

Your notes:_____

_____

_____

_____

#47 - ROMANTIC LOVE

<u>Have you ever been loved by another person?</u>
- By whom?

<u>How did you meet?</u>

<u>What happened?</u>
- Dating
- Marriage
- Break-up, Divorce, Widowhood

<u>Have you ever loved another person?</u>
- Have you had more than one "true love"?

Your notes:_____

_____

_____

_____

❈

_____

"Love Ever After"
by Sallie Ringle

Allen and I were married on May 8, 1966. Once we started dating we knew we were meant for each other, and married after six months. My parents were not in favor of the relationship because we were so young, but agreed to give us a small wedding in northern California.

The Vietnam War was going full storm and Allen did not have a deferment. The draft finally got him, and we were stationed in Germany for two years. Our son Don was born there. Once we returned to the US, Allen couldn't get work. We fought a lot. We were very frustrated and angry with life. My parents got involved and convinced me I needed to end my marriage. I was granted a divorce in 1970. I saw Allen a few times after that and at one point I thought we might be able to work things out. In the end I always got cold feet and was afraid of my parents' reaction. I married again for a second time in 1974.

Jump ahead to 2005. I was going to my son's wedding in San Diego. Both my ex-husbands would be there too. Talk about awkward. I hadn't seen Allen in 35 years. I really wanted to see him, talk to him, be in his presence. I decided I wouldn't be deterred by the awkwardness of the situation. "I know," I said to myself, "I'll ask our son Don." "Don, is Allen here?" "Yea" he replied. "Where?" I asked nonchalantly. I didn't want to give away that I was looking forward to our reunion. Don pointed Allen out to me.

When Allen turned around and I could see him fully, I really ogled. He was always the handsomest man I had ever known, and was still oh so handsome. Tall, 6'4", a shock of white hair that had thinned some, yet looked sexy on him. He was wearing a black suit with black T-shirt under the jacket. Very European looking. I kept watching him and waiting for the opportunity to make a move.

When he walked up to the bar, I sprang into action. "Hi Allen. It's good to see you after all this time. Don told me you were living in the Mariana Islands. Did you know I lived in Singapore for six years?" That was the beginning. I had spoken to the man I had never truly gotten over. The man I had always loved even though I was married to my second husband for 30 years. I loved Mike too. We had two daughters together and made a good life. But Allen had always been in my heart as my first and most true love. Our brief conversation sent butterflies and tingles through me. It was as though the years apart had never been. I felt almost giddy. Yet there was a sadness in me too. I had no idea what would happen after that Saturday in October 2005. Was that the end of us again? After all, he lived in Oregon, a little too far away to have a relationship.

About a month later I got a call from Allen. He said he thought maybe we should get together to talk. My heart started racing. Of course I wanted to meet with him. He was the love of my life. We made a plan that he would come to my house in Lake Arrowhead. I had no idea what would happen. After all, I had divorced him and taken his son away, and even had him give up parental rights so my second husband could adopt our son. I think I had good reason to be extremely anxious. I met Allen at the bottom of the mountain so he could follow me up to my house. I remember driving like a maniac. I wanted to be with him so much.

I made a special dinner. At first we were both tentative, not knowing what the other thought or felt. After dinner and a few glasses of wine we settled down comfortably. We shared our memories. I got out photos and said, "Remember this?" I brought out mementos I had saved from when we were together. The picture of the coast where we honeymooned. A sweater his mother had knit for me. Photographs of our son as a baby in Germany. At some point I giddily leaned over and kissed him on the cheek. Within minutes we were kissing and time stood still. We were passionate for each other. Allen spent that night with me, in fact he spent the next several days with me. Our son Don called Allen several times asking when he was coming to San Diego. All Allen said was, "When I decide to."

It has not been all perfect for us since then. I had a lot to learn about Allen's needs and how to meet them. I still had the bad habit of blurting out whatever came into my mind. I know I hurt his feelings often. But we were willing to work on our relationship and build a future together. At first we thought we would re-marry. I even made a wedding dress. As time passed we realized our relationship was good the way it was. We didn't need to marry.

Allen is devoted to me and I to him. I believe he cherishes me. I never grow tired of his loving touch and little squeezes. We laugh many times every day. He spoils me, doing all the cooking and lots of the cleaning. He understands me and puts up with my defects of character. He has inspired me to become who I am today. I know he has made me a better person over the last ten years. I don't know how many more years we have together, but I know that with Allen I am fulfilled. I am blessed to have found my soul mate again.

#48 - LUCK

<u>Are you a lucky person?</u>
- Write about a time when you were just plain lucky

<u>Was there a time when disaster was averted and a lucky fate seemed to intervene?</u>

Your notes:_____

_____

_____

_____

#49 - HAPPY

<u>Are you happy right now?</u>
- What is making you happy?

Your notes:_____

_____

_____

_____

HELPFUL HINT #7 - AMBIGUITY

Some of the exercises in this book may seem to you to be unclear and ambiguous. They are designed that way. Just as you see and hear and smell things differently than others, what you read into an exercise may be different from what others read into it. Words and phrases have multiple meanings. One word spelled the same way may have two different pronunciations and two different meanings. As you write, think of different responses you can make based on different readings and different interpretations of the same word or phrase.

#50 - UNREQUITED LOVE

<u>Do you have an unrequited love?</u>
- Why were you and this person unable to get together?

<u>Did you ever meet up with this person after your feelings of passion were over? If so, what happened?</u>
- Your old feelings were rekindled
- You admitted to the person your former feelings
- There was no spark

<u>Do you still have feelings for this person?</u>

Your notes:_____

_____

_____

_____

#51 - LOVE YOU

<u>Write a love letter</u>

Your notes:_____

_____

_____

_____

#52 - MARRIAGE

<u>Have you ever been married?</u>
- Have you been married more than once?

<u>Are you married now?</u>
- Separated

- Divorced
- Widowed

How did you meet your spouse(s)?
- Describe your first date

Did you know your spouse was "the one" from the beginning, or did love need time to grow?
- What did you like about this person?
- What did this person like about you?

Describe the proposal and engagement
- Where did the proposal take place?
- What was said?
- Was there a ring?
- Did your family support your choice?

If you had it to do all over again, would you still marry this person?

If you never married (or remarried), why not?

Your notes:_____

_____

_____

_____

❧

"A Day at Dodger Stadium"
by Jeanne Master

On the first Saturday in May it was Presbyterian Day at Dodger Stadium. Our church committed to a number of discounted tickets and a bus to take us there. My grandson Tyson had never seen a major league baseball game, so I decided to take him. I packed a lunch, took plenty of money, and off we went. The year was 1983.

We were enjoying the day and I was totally focused on my grandson when a man seated in front of us became very friendly. I was polite, but not interested in pursuing a friendship. The man kept turning around and talking to me. Later he told me he noticed I was not wearing a wedding ring, and was attracted to me. About the eighth inning he asked me what Presbyterian church I attended. The following Sunday I walked into church with two of my granddaughters. The man was there. He asked the usher my name and said, "She has a lot of kids." The usher, who knew me, answered, "Those are her grandchildren." For several Sundays this man found me on the patio after church to talk.

Finally he asked me out to dinner. I said, "No, but you can take me dancing." We went dancing at Industry Hills. Following that we took seven years of dancing lessons.

We fell in love and were married at our Presbyterian Church on December 26, 1983 with his four adult children and my three adult children in attendance, and my beloved brother, Kenny, giving me away. Two grandsons lit the candles at the church and two granddaughters attended the guest book. A couple of hundred relatives and friends attended, and at the reception we danced and danced.

That Dodger Stadium flirt is still my husband, and we just celebrated our 30th wedding anniversary.

#53 - WEDDING

<u>Describe your wedding(s)</u>
- Venue
- Guests
- Reception

<u>What was your most memorable wedding gift?</u>

<u>Describe your honeymoon(s)</u>

Your notes:_____

_____

_____

_____

#54 - MARRIAGE HOME

<u>Describe the first place you lived as a married couple</u>
<u>Describe the first home you bought as a married couple</u>

Your notes:_____

_____

_____

_____

#55 - REUNION

<u>Write the speech you'd like to give at your high school reunion</u>
- How does the speech you would give at your 10th reunion differ from the speech you'd give at your 30th reunion?

Your notes:_____

_____

_____

_____

#56 - BLESSING (1)

<u>Make a list of your blessings</u>
- Can you find blessings in misfortune, helping you look beyond misfortune to possibility?

Your notes:_____

_____

_____

_____

#57 - BLESSING (2)

<u>Who do you want to bless?</u>
- What are your words of blessing?

Your notes:_____

_____

_____

_____

FOUR

HELPFUL HINT #8 - FILE THINGS AWAY

As the years go by, family stories can go from hurtful to interesting. One of the reasons my great-grandfather came to America as a teenager was to avoid conscription into the army of the Austro-Hungarian Empire. If told too close to the event, this story makes my great-grandfather sound like a draft-dodger who shirked his duty, and may be hurtful. But many years have passed since my great-grandfather's death, and this story is now an interesting part of my family's history and no longer has the power to hurt.

If you have stories you want to record that are an important part of your family's history, but you do not want them included in your autobiography, write them down and put them away in a file to be opened later when your family is ready to hear them or after you are gone. You may want to do this with things you believe could be hurtful or damaging to your family if told now, but should be remembered. Write them down, file them away and let them be read by future generations when they are interesting or quaint, and can no longer cause hurt.

Remember though, sometimes a secret is not yours to tell. Your autobiography is not the place for you to violate confidences or express feelings of rancor and animosity toward your family. You do not want to be remembered as a thoughtless person who violated the privacy of others.

#58 - HERO WORSHIP

<u>Who do you hero worship?</u>
<u>Is there a person you once worshipped, but do not worship any longer?</u>
- What caused this person to fall from favor in your eyes?

Your notes:_____

_____

_____

_____

#59 - REFUGE

<u>Where do you take refuge?</u>
- When do you feel the need for refuge?

Your notes:_____

_____

_____

_____

#60 - SEXY YOU

<u>Write an erotic story in which you are the star</u>

Your notes:_____

_____

_____

_____

#61 - SEX

How and when did you learn about sex?
- Where did you think babies came from before you learned the truth?
- What were your original ideas about sex?

How did you feel when you first learned the truth?
- Horror
- Curiosity
- Shock
- Amusement
- Disbelief
- Or?

Your notes:_____

_____

_____

_____

#62 - DEFAULT

What is your default setting?

Your notes:_____

_____

_____

_____

#63 - HELPLESS

When do you feel helpless?

Your notes:_____

_____

_____

_____

#64 - BECAUSE

In one of our autobiography classes we wrote about our favorite outfits. Jeanne B. wrote about a black dress and matching hat she bought, "Because I could."

After class I thought a lot about that phrase - "because I could". It tells so much and could describe so many things: triumph over difficulties, adventures, things you bought or vacations you took, surviving an illness, changes in money, relationship, or financial status, or something you did against all odds.

<u>Write about something you did "because you could"</u>
<u>What does this phrase mean to you?</u>
- The freedom to make choices that comes with being an adult
- Coming through a difficulty, challenging time, or illness
- Change in monetary, residence, or relationship status allowing you to do something, buy something, or go somewhere that was not previously possible
- Finding a source of inner courage or strength
- A chance to have an adventure
- Having a new sense of independence
- Or?

<u>How did it make you feel to do something because you could?</u>

Your notes:_____

_____

_____

_____

※

"The Simple Black Dress"
by Jeanne Behr

The year was 1955 in Denver, Colorado. I had just graduated from high school and found a job at the Mountain States Telephone Company in downtown Denver. It was a fun job working with women my own age.

During my lunch hour or after work, I would shop at the big name department stores nearby. One day I found a simple black dress and hat. I could wear them on dates and to church. Being young and single, I bought them because I could! As life moved on after marriage and children, moments of "Because I could" were few and far between, if ever again!

By the way - I still have the dress.

※

#65 - BETTER THAN

<u>What is there nothing better than in your world?</u>
- "There is nothing better than … "

Your notes:_____
_____
_____
_____

#66 - TOO MANY

<u>You can't have too many what?</u>

Your notes:_____
_____
_____
_____

#67 - MOMENT

<u>Describe your Big Moment</u>

Your notes:_____
_____
_____
_____

#68 - SCENE

<u>Describe a time when you left the scene</u>

Your notes:_____

_____

_____

_____

HELPFUL HINT #9 - DON'T GET DISTRACTED

Don't let minutia distract you or keep you from writing. While it is important to find a comfortable place to write, wallpapering your writing nook or organizing your pens or waiting to begin writing until you have bought the perfect notebook or the right paper or the latest computer is not the same thing as writing. <u>You</u> make your autobiography, not finding the perfect piece of pretty paper.

#69 - HOW DO YOU LOOK?

<u>Describe the way you look</u>
- Hair and eye color
- Height
- Body type
- Your best physical feature

<u>Who were you told you looked like when you were younger?</u>
- Your mother or father
- A sibling or other family member
- Someone famous

<u>If you could change one thing about your physical appearance, what would it be?</u>

Your notes:_____

_____

_____

_____

#70 - PHOTOS

<u>Go through your photos and select a picture of yourself</u>
- Why did you select this photo?
- What about this photo appeals to you?
- When and where was this photo taken?
- What story does it tell?

<u>How do you look in this photo?</u>
- Were you surprised by the way you looked when you first saw this photo?
- Do you look differently in this photo than you thought you looked when it was taken?
- Do you look better? Worse?

Your notes:_____

_____

_____

_____

#71 - DROP THE REINS

"He acquired the use of a discarded donkey, saying, as he let the reins fall and gave the beast its head, settling himself on its back, and taking out a pencil and a manuscript book: 'Go where thou wilt my friend. I confine myself to thy taste and good behavior.' "

- Eleanor Calhoun -

<u>Where is your donkey taking you?</u>
- Is this a real place or an imaginary place?
- Where are you when you mount up?
- Is this a physical destination or a state of mind?
- Is this destination in the past, the present, or the future?

<u>Is it difficult for you to trust your donkey?</u>
- Is your imaginary donkey more headstrong than you expected?

As you do this exercise, try to use your imagination and not let your writing be trapped by logic. Think freely and throw yourself into it. Let your donkey fly through space and time. Just start writing and have some fun.

Your notes:_____

_____

_____

_____

#72 - ROOMIES

With whom, besides a spouse, have you shared a room, apartment, or house?
- College roommate
- Sharing with friends
- Renting a room in someone's house
- Sharing with a sibling or other relative
- Sharing with a traveling companion

How did you get along with your roommate(s)?
- Was there anything about your roommate(s) that drove you crazy?
- Did you drive your roommate(s) crazy?

Are you still friends?

Your notes:_____

_____

_____

_____

#73 - TAKING THE TEST

What is the most difficult test you ever took?
- School
- Professional licensing, i.e. Bar exam, medical boards, nursing or CPA exam
- Skilled trade licensing exam, i.e. electrician, beautician, plumber
- Citizenship exam
- Driving test
- Or?

How did you prepare?

Did you pass?
- If you failed the first time, how did you prepare to ensure you passed when you took it again?

What made it difficult for you?
- Subject matter was challenging

- The pressure to pass was too intense
- You didn't care enough to adequately prepare
- Or?

Your notes:_____

_____

_____

_____

#74 - SMILE

<u>What makes you smile?</u>

Your notes:_____

_____

_____

_____

#75 - PROCRASTINATE

<u>Are you a procrastinator?</u>
- What are you putting off until tomorrow that you should do today?
<u>Will you eventually get around to doing these things?</u>

Your notes:_____

_____

_____

_____

HELPFUL HINT #10 - CURING PROCRASTINATION

If you're anything like me, sometimes all the advice and all the helpful hints in the world just don't work. Sometimes you <u>**JUST DON'T WANT TO DO IT**</u>!

Based on my experience as a world-class procrastinator, I have developed some techniques to get myself moving. You may find them helpful.

- Try to make writing something you <u>want</u> to do, not something you <u>have</u> to do. If you make your writing enjoyable, you will be less likely to procrastinate.

- When I am tempted to procrastinate, I tell myself I won't want to do it tomorrow any more than I want to do it right now, so I might as well do it today because then I won't lose sleep fretting, and I can congratulate myself for doing something I really did not want to do. For some reason this works for me.

- Break up your project into more manageable pieces by setting small tasks and deadlines for yourself.

- Start with the easiest part of your project. This will get you in the habit of writing, and give you the satisfaction of completing a task.

- Eliminate distractions and find a place to write where you can concentrate.

- Do not let fear of making mistakes stop you. In writing your autobiography it is almost impossible for you to make mistakes, because this is <u>your</u> story, and how you tell your story is right for you. You only fail when you don't do it at all.

- Do not defeat yourself by being a perfectionist. Getting started and moving forward should be your goal. You can make corrections later during editing.

- If a way of doing a task stops working for you, even if it "always" worked before, look for a new approach so you can move on and achieve your goal.

- When you are tempted to give up, keep at your task for just five minutes more. I find that when I give myself permission to stop after five minutes, I usually get involved in what I'm doing, and end up working for hours, not just minutes, more.

- It is easy to convince yourself that you're being productive when you're actually just doing busy work. Spending time making "to do" lists will not automatically help you accomplish your goal. Use lists only if they help you get started doing productive work.

- Make a commitment to yourself to finish what you start.

#76 - COUNTRY

<u>If you were a country, what country would you be?</u>
- Why?

Your notes:_____

_____

_____

_____

#77 - FEAST

Ernest Hemingway once described life as a "moveable feast"

<u>Has your life been a moveable feast or something a bit less tasty?</u>

Your notes:_____

_____

_____

_____

#78 - GOT AWAY

<u>Describe the "one that got away"</u>
- Love
- Job
- Opportunity
- Or?

Your notes:_____

_____

_____

_____

#79 - NECESSARY

===

"It is no use saying, 'We are doing our best.' You have got to succeed in doing what is necessary."

- WINSTON CHURCHILL -

===

<u>When did you succeed in doing what was necessary?</u>
- What did you do?

Your notes:_____

_____

_____

_____

#80 - REVISION

<u>If you could rewrite your personal history, what would you do differently?</u>
- How do you think doing things differently would have changed your life?

Your notes:_____

_____

_____

_____

#81 - AGAIN

<u>Describe your recurring dreams</u>

Your notes:_____

_____

_____

_____

#82 - MOTHERS

You may find this exercise difficult and very emotional. Even when memories of your mother are happy, there may still be sadness because the experiences you had with your mother are over, and will not happen again. My mother had a very close relationship with her mom, and although she has many happy memories, she still finds it difficult to write about them. Her mother died much too young, and Mom still grieves, even though her mother has been gone for over 60 years. With one's mother - mine, yours, anyone's - there is bound to be longing for what you had, thoughts about what you wish had been, regrets, happiness, joy, sorrow, grief - you name it - the whole range of emotions.

If you find writing about <u>your</u> mother too difficult, try writing about <u>you</u> as a mother. It doesn't have to be about mothering your own children. You can write about giving motherly advice to someone.

You can write about mothering animals, or about you doing something for someone else's mother. I have a <u>great</u> mother and love her dearly, but when I did this exercise, I wrote about a time in which I had the privilege and honor of "mothering" another person at the end of her life.

"Mothering" is not limited to women with children. "Mothering" is not limited to women. We all have the ability to mother when we nurture and care.

<u>Write a Mother's Day message</u>
<u>You may write a message to:</u>
- Your mother (or the mother figure) who raised you
- A friend who acted as a mother to you
- The mother of your children or grandchildren
- Someone who gave you motherly advice
- The mother you wish you had
- Yourself

<u>Here are some suggestions</u>
- Write about a Mother's Day card or gift you gave to your mother
- Write about a Mother's Day card or gift you received from your children or grandchildren
- Write the Mother's Day card you wish you had sent to your mother
- Write the Mother's Day card you wish you had received from your children
- Write about a time you were mothered when you really needed it

Your notes:_____

_____

_____

_____

#83 - SIBLINGS

<u>Who are your siblings?</u>
- Brothers
- Sisters

- Half and step siblings

Were you close to your siblings when you were growing up?
- What did you do with your siblings when you were children?
- What did you fight about with your siblings when you were children?

Are you close to your siblings now?
- What do you do with your siblings now?

If you are estranged from any of your siblings, what caused the estrangement?
- Is there any chance of reconciliation?

Which sibling are you **most** like? Why?

Which sibling are you **least** like? Why?

Your notes:_____

_____

_____

_____

#84 - MORE LOVE

Other than a human or animal, what do you really love?

Tangible things, for example:
- Electronics (TV, computer, phone, Kindle)
- Car
- Shoes
- A country or city

Intangible things, for example:
- Music
- Art
- A certain sensory experience or sensation
- A talent or characteristic of yours
- Travel

Concepts, for example:
- Freedom
- God

Your notes:_____

_____

_____

_____

❧

"First Love"
by Robert Hamer

Neither my father nor my uncle were pool players. My cousin and I were not taught how to handle the stick, or about eight ball, or rotation, or when to chalk the tip, or (heaven forbid) ever taken to a pool hall. It was 1936, I was twelve years old, and I wanted a pool table.

"What do you want for Christmas?" my mother asked me one dark winter afternoon as she prepared dinner.

I was sitting at the kitchen table watching her peel potatoes. I replied, "A pool table." She must have cringed.

She moved in silence from sink to refrigerator and refrigerator to stove. "That's nice," she said. "Perhaps."

From Thanksgiving to mid-December she asked repeatedly what I wanted for Christmas.

"A pool table," was my unvarying response.

In anticipation of my gift, my cousin Bruce and I spent those pre-holiday weeks making plans to spend Christmas Day shooting pool. It didn't matter that neither of us were experienced at the game. We knew we could teach each other. At the age of twelve the details of where to play, how to play, or when to play were trifles. They just didn't matter.

The Christmas tree was purchased and decorated six days before Santa's scheduled arrival, and gaily wrapped presents began to appear. First one and then a couple more, each with a card addressed to Jane or Bob or Dad or Mother. In addition to those gifts, there was always a major gift from Santa which would mysteriously appear after my sister and I had gone to bed on Christmas Eve. I was confident that sometime after bedtime, my folks would retrieve my pool table from its hiding place and install it under the tree.

Early Christmas morning my sister Jane came into my bedroom and together we went downstairs and entered the living room. We had already guessed what was in the wrapped packages, so it was the big surprises that excited us. I looked eagerly for the green felt of my pool table.

We stopped at the living room door. I was astounded to see a bike. A shiny new red and white bike with a wire basket attached to the handle bars, balloon tires, coaster brakes and red reflectors on the rear fender.

A bike. The delight of it made me shiver. I wanted to ride it NOW!

After breakfast, Mother and Dad let me go outside to try out my new bike. There were a few spills, but soon I mastered the skill of riding a two wheeler, and rode down the block to show Bruce. He had also received a red two wheeler for Christmas. My aunt greeted me from their front porch, roaring with laughter, because she had been a co-conspirator to both surprises.

I had that red bike until I enlisted in the Navy. I rode it to parks, to see girls, to the river, to music lessons - everywhere. Sometimes with Bruce, sometimes alone, but everywhere.

I loved that bike - and it sure was a lot better than a pool table.

#85 - TALENT

<u>What are your talents?</u>
<u>What things do you have absolutely NO talent for?</u>
- What talents do you wish you had?

Your notes:_____

_____

_____

_____

#86 - LIGHTER

<u>Do you have a light heart?</u>
- How is your heart light?
- If your heart is heavy, what could you do to have a lighter heart?

<u>Is your heart lighter now than when you were younger?</u>

Your notes:_____

_____

_____

_____

#87 - WISE

Who is the wisest person you know?
- What bit of wisdom has this person given to you?

Your notes:_____

_____

_____

_____

#88 - INFLUENCE

Who had the greatest influence on you when you were growing up?
- What did this person say or do that was so influential?

Was this person a continuing influence, or was their influence the result of a single incident?

How did this person's influence impact you?
- Does this person's influence continue to impact you?
- Was this person's influence positive or negative?

Your notes:_____

_____

_____

_____

"My Granddad"
by Aurora Reinhart

My mom's father was my Granddad Eliseo Hernandez. I loved him dearly. Today, as days go by I feel that his image in my mind is slowly fading away. I am afraid I will lose his handsome debonair image. It's sad there were no pictures taken of him. Life was difficult then, and picture taking was the last thing they would spend money on. I am thankful I have this chance to try to recreate his image, his beautiful home and garden, his simple and contented life. According to my parents he was <u>soooo</u> happy when I was born. I was his first granddaughter and the first to survive. My first two brothers had died in infancy. I loved spending my summer vacations with him. As soon as school closed for summer, he took a bus to our house in Manila, spent a few days for a visit, and then took me back with him to the province where he lived.

His house was located in the Pampanga region of the Philippines in a small barrio called San Antonio. The house had a nipa roof, varnished bamboo beams, wooden walls, varnished bamboo flooring and large windows. The house was huge and the rooms airy. The Philippines has a tropical climate, hot and humid. His house was well ventilated and comfortable. I loved walking barefooted on the smooth shiny floors that were kept clean and shiny by being polished with dry banana leaves. We ate in a corner by the dining room and sat on the floor. The dining table had twelve inch legs (like Japanese tables). We ate with our cleaned washed hands. I enjoyed those meals. He always had a story to tell as we ate. On the other side of the room was a formal dining table that seated twenty people which he also built. This table was used during fiestas and special events, when the formal seating arrangements and accessories were dug out of the chest, cleaned, polished and arranged.

There were no ovens or electric stoves. Cooking was a big task. People had to collect wood and build kindling before the fire could start. I saw my aunt and step-grandmom blowing and fanning before the kindling got started. My granddad built a two burner concrete stove. I called it The Beast. It had a funnel for rice husk fuel. He got the rice husks from a nearby mill. The ashes from the burned rice husks were funneled down through a pipe that went through the flooring to the ground. The ashes were used to clean pots and pans. "Comet Cleanser" in today's world.

In the front yard was a line of beadle nut trees. The nuts were collected by my grandfather. He chewed a piece after each meal. There were also lots of flowers in the front yard. We were obliged to take siestas every day after lunch, but sometimes my uncle and I escaped through the veranda and got lost in the garden.

My grandfather passed away when I was 16 years old. I was beyond myself. I missed him dearly, and miss him even now. I am truly glad I will remember him again every time I read this short story I wrote about him.

#89 - COLLECTING

<u>What do you collect?</u>
- As a child
- As a young adult
- In middle age
- Now

<u>Why do you collect these things?</u>
- What about them attracts you?

<u>Are there any things you've stopped collecting? Why?</u>
- What did you do with your collection?

Your notes:_____

_____

_____

_____

#90 - CITY

<u>What is your favorite city?</u>
- What is it about this city that you love?

Your notes:_____

_____

_____

_____

#91 - PRECIOUS

<u>In what way is your life precious to you?</u>
- If it does not feel precious to you right now, what can you do to make it precious to you in the future?

Your notes:_____

_____

_____

_____

#92 - NEED

<u>What is it you **really** need?</u>

Your notes:_____

_____

_____

_____

FIVE

The autobiography process can be hard, and may bring up many emotions. Part of the process is being comfortable telling <u>your</u> story in <u>your</u> way with <u>your</u> voice. Speaking with your true voice is part of your legacy. The story of your life deserves to be told, and it deserves to be told as <u>you</u> want to tell it. When you stay with it, even when it becomes difficult, it says a lot about your strength and your perseverance.

I hope you find the autobiography experience meaningful, and have fun with the exercises. As you do this, you may find some things are very hard. Be nice to yourself. If something is too difficult, put it aside and come back to it later. Look at the things that make you smile, and put away the difficult things for another time. The more you write and the longer you do this, the easier it will get.

I promise!!

#93 - HOBBIES

<u>What are your hobbies?</u>
- As a child?

- As a busy young adult?
- In middle age?
- Now?

Your notes:_____

_____

_____

_____

#94 - SIMPLE THINGS

Sometimes it is not the big or important things that evoke memories. Sometimes it is a simple thing like the wooden spoon your mother always used when she made a cake or the sweater your dad always wore when he watched a football game.

<u>Look around your house, and find a simple thing that evokes a memory</u>
- Write about this item and your memory

Your notes:_____

_____

_____

_____

#95 - WORK AND CAREER (1)

<u>Describe your working life</u>
- Paid and unpaid jobs
- Homemaker or work outside the home
- First job
- Part-time jobs
- Summer jobs

Describe your career path
- Jobs you applied for and did not get
- Jobs you loved
- Jobs you hated
- Jobs you quit
- Jobs you lost – fired or laid off

Your employers
- The best company you ever worked for? Why?
- The worst company you ever worked for? Why?
- Your best boss or supervisor? Why?
- Your worst boss or supervisor? Why?

How were you able to use your special talents on the job?
- What were you really good at on the job?

What was the favorite of all your jobs?

What was the job that "got away"?
- Was there a job you did not take (either refused an offer or no offer was made), that had you taken it, may have changed your career path?

Your notes:_____

_____

_____

_____

#96 - WORK AND CAREER (2)

Were you ever mentored?
- Who mentored you?

Did you ever mentor another employee?
- Who did you mentor?

Did having or not having a mentor change your career path?

Your notes:_____

_____

_____

_____

#97 - WORK AND CAREER (3)

<u>What makes you proudest when you think about your working life?</u>
- Accomplishments
- Promotions and raises
- Innovations you created
- Triumph over difficult situations
- Friendships

<u>What regrets do you have about your working life?</u>

Your notes:_____

_____

_____

_____

#98 - WORK AND CAREER (4)

<u>Have you ever been fired from a job?</u>
- What reasons were you given for being fired?
- In your opinion, what is the real reason you were fired?

<u>Was the firing expected or unexpected?</u>

<u>What did you do after you were fired?</u>
- Collect unemployment
- File a grievance or lawsuit
- Get depressed and go into hiding
- Promptly find another job

- Move
- Or?

<u>In retrospect, do you think the firing was justified?</u>

Your notes:_____

_____

_____

_____

#99 - DREAM JOB

<u>Describe your dream job or career</u>
- Describe the job you always believed you'd be great doing

<u>Did you actually get this dream job or have this dream career?</u>
- Did the reality of having this dream job live up to your expectations?

<u>If you were not able to have this dream job, why not?</u>
- Too costly to pursue the required education
- Feelings of insecurity and doubt
- Time Issues
- Family issues
- Fitness or physical ability limitations
- You did what was "right" or "sensible"
- Other commitments
- Or?

Your notes:_____

_____

_____

_____

#100 - SIXTH SENSE

Have you ever had an experience of extra sensory perception (ESP)?
- Was it something you sensed or something another person sensed about you?
- Did the thing you sensed (or that was sensed about you) actually happen?

Do you often experience ESP?

Your notes:_____

_____

_____

_____

#101 - *DÉJÀ VU*

Déjà vu is the feeling of having experienced before something that is actually happening for the first time.

Describe a time when you experienced *déjà vu*

Your notes:_____

_____

_____

_____

#102 - SPECIAL DAY

Tell the story of a special day in your life
- A special birthday
- The day you fell in love
- Your wedding day
- Birth of a child or grandchild

- Graduation
- A day during an important trip
- The first day of a job
- The most beautiful sight you've ever seen
- The best meal you ever ate
- The first time
- First day at school or university
- A day you survived danger
- A day you received a difficult diagnosis
- A day you triumphed
- Your luckiest day

Your notes:_____

_____

_____

_____

HELPFUL HINT #12 - USE DIALOG

Try opening your story with a conversation. In the quote below, notice how time, place, activity, and opinion are established by just a few lines of dialog.

"Fifteen-two, fifteen-four, and a pair are six," my uncle said to my dad as they played cribbage at the kitchen table. Then he added, "The country will never elect him again." I was 12 years-old, and it was the presidential campaign of 1936.

My dad and Uncle Oren drank beer, played cards, and discussed politics close to the Servel, which had replaced our ice box in the early 1930s.

"Fifteen-two, fifteen-four, three are seven and his nibs makes eight," counted my dad. "He's an autocrat."

Dad picked up, sorted his cards, played the seven and repeated, "Damn Democrat." I was well into my teens before I learned that "Democrat" was not a two word term. Never did Dad nor my uncle refer to them as anything other than "Damn Democrats."

Neither they nor their wives nor their parents had ever voted for a Democrat. Or if they had, they never openly admitted it. They remained Republicans in 1940. In 1944, I was in the Navy, but I doubt their politics had changed. The first year I could vote in a presidential election was 1948. Dad compared for me Truman's vices with Dewey's virtues.

"Thank God," he said. "The war is over and now we can clean up the mess in Washington."

I listened to Dad, and hesitated. I had something difficult to say.

"Dad," I choked out, "there's something I have to tell you. I have registered as a Democrat. Does that make any difference between us?"

A long silence followed. Perhaps a tear welled up in his eye.

Then he replied, "Never!!"

- BILL SHEARER -

#103 - DIALOG

Practice writing dialog
- Create a dialog between yourself and another person
- Create a dialog between yourself and a thing
- Create a dialog between yourself and a situation
- Create a dialog between yourself and a place
- Create a dialog between different parts of yourself

Your notes:_____

_____

_____

_____

#104 - CHEATED

Did you ever feel cheated out of something you felt you deserved?
- A prize or award
- A raise or promotion
- An honor or commendation
- A scholarship
- An elected position
- Or?

Why do you believe this happened?

Your notes:_____

_____

_____

_____

#105 - CHARITY

<u>Are you a charitable person?</u>
<u>What are your special causes?</u>
- Children
- Environment
- Animals
- Religion
- Health related issues

<u>Did you develop any charitable interests as a result of personal experience or the experience of someone close to you?</u>
- Fundraising for medical research after facing your own or a loved one's health issues
- Donations to animal protection after adopting a shelter animal
- Donations in memory of a loved one

Your notes:_____

_____

_____

_____

#106 - BABIES

<u>Are you a "baby" person?</u>
<u>What baby has meant the most to you?</u>
- First child
- First grandchild
- First daughter
- First son
- Someone else's baby who made you think you might want your own child
- A puppy or kitten

How did you feel the first time you held a baby?

Your notes:_____

_____

_____

_____

❧

"The First Time I Held A Baby"
by Susan Fraizer

The first baby I remember holding was my sister Carol. She was so small. She only weighed four pounds and a few ounces when she was born. She was fussed over quite a bit by my grandfather and me. I thought she was the cutest baby ever. She had white blond hair and the biggest blue eyes. Her hair was so fuzzy and white that you had to look really hard to see it. My grandfather would let me hold her when I sat on the couch in the living room. She hardly moved and her cries were so soft. She had a hard time as she coughed a lot. She made it though, and I am so thankful for that. My mother would put her bassinet deep in the closet. It really bothered me that she was way back in the dark. I sneaked in there all the time to check on her. I adored being her big sister.

I found my sister Carol to be such a joy in my life. I watched over her and loved every moment of it. My two other sisters were not thrilled with her and were mean to her. She was not as strong as the rest of us. When she was old enough to ride a tricycle she could not keep up with the three of us on our bicycles. The other two called her names and I would chase them away. She would still try to keep up on her tricycle. I would get off my bicycle and hold on to the handle bars of the trike with her and scoot my foot on the pavement to help her go faster. She would squeal with delight at being able to keep up. That is what it is like to this day. Always standing together.

We are best friends and there is nothing that could ever come between us.   I feel God blessed me in giving me such a beautiful sister.

#107 - HOLIDAYS

<u>What is your favorite holiday?</u>
<u>What are your family's holiday traditions?</u>
- What food is eaten, who is invited, where is the celebration held, what is done to celebrate?
- Special songs, games, music, decorations, readings (i.e. scripture)

<u>Do your celebrations blend traditions from more than one culture?</u>
<u>How have these celebrations changed from your birth family to your adult family?</u>
- What holidays did you celebrate as a child that you no longer celebrate?

<u>What traditions did you create?</u>
- Family traditions you changed and adapted in adulthood
- Traditions that are a blending of your birth family's traditions and the family traditions of your spouse or partner
- New traditions you adapted from the celebrations of friends

<u>Describe the best holiday you ever had</u>
<u>Describe the worst holiday you ever had</u>

Your notes:_____

_____

_____

_____

_____

#108 - SPECIAL FOOD

What are the special recipes, meals, or foods you and your family have for special celebrations and special occasions?
- As a child?
- As an adult?

Your notes:_____

_____

_____

_____

#109 - CRAZY

Have you ever had a crazy money making scheme?
- What was it?

Did you try to implement your scheme?
- What happened?

Your notes:_____

_____

_____

_____

#110 - DON'T

What don't you believe?
- What happened to cause your disbelief?

Your notes:_____

_____

_____

_____

❧

_____

HELPFUL HINT #13 - CONDUCT AN INTERVIEW

Interview a family member or friend. Ask about their memories of you - after all, this is your story. But remember, you don't live in a vacuum, so ask them for their memories of their own lives. Their lives have touched yours and help complete your story.

_____

❧

#111 - PAST LIFE

<u>Have you ever had an experience or feeling leading you to believe that you led a past life?</u>
<u>Have you ever been hypnotized and done a past life regression?</u>
- Describe your past life

Your notes:_____

_____

_____

_____

#112 - DAYDREAM

<u>What do you daydream about?</u>
- How have your daydreams changed as you've aged?

Your notes:_____

_____

_____

_____

#113 - DREAM

<u>Write about a time when your dreams came true</u>

Your notes:_____

_____

_____

_____

#114 - BAD DREAM

<u>Write about a bad dream you remember</u>
- From your childhood
- From your adulthood
- Recently

<u>What do you think this bad dream is trying to tell you?</u>

Your notes:_____

_____

_____

_____

#115 - ATTITUDE

<u>Are you an</u>
- Optimist
- Pessimist
- Realist
- Pragmatist

<u>Why?</u>

Your notes:_____

_____

_____

_____

#116 - PUTTERING

<u>What do you do when you putter?</u>

Your notes:_____

_____

_____

_____

#117 - GOLD

<u>Give yourself a gold star</u>
- What did you do to earn your gold star?

Your notes:_____

_____

_____

_____

#118 - HEIRLOOM

<u>If you could choose one family heirloom to be yours, what would it be?</u>
- Jewelry
- Furniture
- Artwork
- Silver
- Family letters or other documents
- Or?

<u>What is the history of this heirloom in your family?</u>
<u>Why did you choose this particular thing?</u>
- If you don't have a family heirloom, what item of yours do you plan to pass down to your family that will become a family heirloom?

Your notes:_____

_____

_____

_____

#119 - YEAR END (1)

<u>How do you feel as one year ends and a new year begins?</u>
- Is there a customary way you and your family "ring out the old" and "ring in the new"?

Your notes:_____

_____

_____

_____

SIX

HELPFUL HINT #14 - BE TRUSTWORTHY

This is your story, and you are entitled to tell it from your point of view. After all, part of the reason for telling your story is because you have things you want to say in your own way, and not parrot the beliefs, philosophies, or experiences of others.

Your perception of events feels true to you because it's your opinion and your viewpoint. But, your beliefs are not necessarily based on fact. Your truth may be based on a false interpretation, a misunderstanding, or a misremembering of events. You may not always remember events accurately, but you need to be trustworthy. Record what you honestly believe happened, but don't infer and don't lie.

#120 - PARK

<u>Describe your favorite park</u>
- National park

- Neighborhood park
- Amusement park
- City park
- Vacant lot
- Wild or undeveloped area

<u>Describe a special memory of this park</u>

Your notes:_____

_____

_____

_____

#121 - COMPASSION

<u>When do you feel compassion?</u>
<u>What do you do to show your compassion?</u>
- For people
- For animals
- For the world

Your notes:_____

_____

_____

_____

#122 - CLOTHES

<u>What was your favorite outfit?</u>
- What made it so special?

<u>Describe an occasion when this outfit was worn</u>
- How did you feel when you wore it?

<u>What happened to this outfit?</u>
- Gave it to someone else
- Donated it
- Sold it at a garage sale or on consignment
- You still have it
- You still have it and still wear it

Your notes:_____

_____

_____

_____

#123 - ROAD TRIP

<u>Describe the first road trip you took in which you were the driver</u>
- Where did you go?
- Did you go by yourself or with others?
- How many miles did you travel?
- How long were you away from home?

<u>Why did you choose this particular destination?</u>

<u>How did you feel as you drove away from home?</u>
- Excited
- Nervous
- Scared
- Eager
- Happy
- Lighthearted
- Adventurous
- Daring
- Grown-up
- Or?

Your notes:_____

_____

_____

_____

#124 - MY MISSION

<u>What is the mission statement for your life that sums up your hopes, goals, and aspirations?</u>
<u>Has your mission statement changed or remained the same throughout your life?</u>
*   If it has changed, what changes did you make and why?

Your notes:_____

_____

_____

_____

#125 - SPORTING LIFE

<u>What is your favorite sport?</u>
*   To play?
*   To watch?

Your notes:_____

_____

_____

_____

"Athletic Prowess"
by Robert Hamer

In 1956 golf was not a serious recreational pursuit. My own clubs came third hand from my father who got them second hand from my uncle. I played infrequently on public courses and never took lessons. My skill level had not risen above inept.

My employer belonged to a business association which held a fun-fest once a year with golf in the morning, late afternoon gin rummy and libations, and concluded with dinner and an awards presentation. My boss made it clear that participation was part of my job description.

On a warm spring morning, thirty foursomes were to tee-off at Riviera Country Club. My own shot left the first tee straight and true, but then ever so gently started to curve right, finally hitting the ground after making a complete right turn. The short shots were not much better, but enough of an improvement to be less hazardous to others in the foursome, on the course, and all animal and bird life. My strokes per hole ranged from eight to ten, and only the par threes saved me from high single and low double digits on every hole.

The tee for the eighteenth fairway at Riviera is at the bottom of a modestly steep hill. The green and cup are at the top of the hill. Neither are visible from the tee. A twenty foot tall periscope allows a golfer on the eighteenth tee to see if the preceding foursome has cleared the green. I was the last in our foursome to tee-off. My ball hit the side of the hill and rolled back down a third of the way. My second shot hit further up the hill and again rolled back. Finally the hill was ascended, the green achieved, and the hole and round completed, at last answering my companions' prayers to the Almighty.

That evening trophies were awarded to players for low net, low gross, and to the winner. My name was called to receive the award for high gross. I opened the booby prize in front of the cat-calling and abusive audience.

I had shot 151.

#126 - IMPORTANT THINGS

<u>What are the ten most important things in your life?</u>
- Most important things when you were growing up
- Most important things as a young adult
- Most important things now

Your notes:_____

_____

_____

_____

#127 - DRINK

<u>Do you drink?</u>
- Never
- Seldom
- Only socially
- To excess

<u>What experiences impacted your decisions about drinking?</u>
- You enjoy a social drink with friends
- You consider yourself a connoisseur
- Family history of alcohol abuse
- Observation of drunken behavior of others
- Shame or embarrassment over your own drunken behavior
- Religious convictions
- You just don't like the taste
- Or?

Your notes:_____

_____

_____

_____

#128 - DRUNK

<u>Describe a time when you were really drunk</u>

Your notes:_____

_____

_____

_____

#129 - WHAT'S YOUR SIGN

<u>What is your sign of the zodiac?</u>
<u>What are the characteristics of your sign?</u>
- Is your personality "typical" of your sign?

Your notes:_____

_____

_____

_____

#130 - SUPERSTITIOUS

<u>What superstitions do you have?</u>

Your notes:_____

_____

_____

_____

#131 - DRIVING

How, when, and where did you learn to drive a car?
Describe your first car
- Did your first car have a name?

Describe any car accidents you had
- Caused by you
- Caused by others

If you never learned to drive or no longer drive, what was the reason for your decision?

Your notes:_____

_____

_____

_____

❈

HELPFUL HINT #15 - IT'S NOT ALL ABOUT YOU

Beware of too much "I, I, I" and "me, me, me". While it is true that this is your story, you don't live in a bubble. You meet other people and are impacted by them. If you are not honest about the roles others play in your life, if it is too much "I, I, I" and "me, me, me", then you are not telling your whole story.

To control too much self-absorption, every so often practice writing as an observer.
- Write about something you've seen, but not <u>your</u> reaction to seeing it
- Put yourself in another person's place, and write from that person's perspective
- Describe an unfamiliar place <u>without</u> describing how you felt being there

#132 - SORRY (1)

<u>Who do you want to say "I'm sorry" to?</u>
- What did you do or not do that makes you sorry?
- What did you say or not say that makes you sorry?

<u>Did you ever apologize?</u>
- If you did apologize, how was it received?
- If you did not apologize, what is preventing you from doing so?

<u>Are you able to apologize now?</u>

Your notes:_____

_____

_____

_____

#133 - SORRY (2)

<u>When do you feel sorry for yourself?</u>

Your notes:_____

_____

_____

_____

#134 - JEALOUSY

<u>What makes you jealous?</u>
- People with nicer homes, cars, or other possessions
- People with more professional success
- People with personality characteristics you admire
- People you consider more attractive
- People with lots of friends
- People with loving spouses and successful children
- Or?

<u>How do you act when you feel jealous?</u>
<u>How do you cope with your feelings of jealousy in order to get past them?</u>

Your notes:_____

_____

_____

_____

#135 - PARENTING

<u>Do you have children?</u>
- Biological and adopted children
- Step children
- Foster children

<u>What are the names of your children?</u>
- Why were they given these names?
- What are their nicknames?

<u>Write a little about each of your children</u>
- Their character
- Their accomplishments
- What makes you proud
- A favorite toy or activity of each child
- A memory of each child that makes you smile

<u>Which parent does each child take after?</u>
- How are each of your children like you?
- How are each of your children like one another?
- How are each of your children different from one another?

<u>What did you do right as a parent?</u>
- What do you believe you could have done better or wish you had done differently as a parent?

<u>Have you lost a child through death or estrangement?</u>
- What did you do to cope with your loss?

Your notes:_____

_____

_____

_____

❧

"My Idea of What I Needed to do as a Parent"
by Susan Fraizer

As I see it, the work of a parent is to teach their children to be strong, kind, and a thing of beauty to the world. To have a meaning in the world, a purpose, is the most important accomplishment they will ever have. Whatever gift your child has, God has given to you to nurture, and you must be responsible for it.

It is almost in one sense as if as a parent you have your child's ties as they are growing up always tied to the foundation of you. It is as if your children are to one day be butterflies. You watch and guide them as they are born from the cocoon stage. You provide opportunities for them to feed and grow in the knowledge of life. They must find what is meaningful and fulfilling to each of them as a person.

One day as their lives unfold, they begin to have wings that start to support their flight. As time goes on they try, still tied to the foundation of your family, to learn how to fly. Each time they try they get stronger and stronger until as a parent it is your ultimate pleasure to be able to let go of them, to set them free in the world. You want to see them soar with the strongest of wings into the world. This is accomplished by the practice they have done all of their lives. And as you set them free, they have an inner beauty and strength to pass on to the rest of the world. The love you have for them can set them free.

#136 - SCAR (1)

<u>What is the story behind a scar your child has?</u>
- How did you feel the first time your child had an injury that left a scar?

Your notes:_____

_____

_____

_____

#137 - NON-PARENTING

<u>If you never had children, why not?</u>
- You're just not a "kid" person and never wanted children
- You wanted children but it was never the "right time"
- There were physical or biological impediments
- You never met the person with whom you wanted to have children
- Or?

<u>If you did not have children, do you have a "substitute"?</u>
- Niece, nephew, or Godchild
- A friend's child
- Pet

<u>If you did not have children, do you now regret that decision?</u>

Your notes:_____

_____

_____

_____

#138 - KNOWLEDGE

<u>What do you know to be true about yourself?</u>
<u>What do you know to be true about other people that you do not know about yourself?</u>
- You may not know how you come across to other people. You're shy but people perceive you as aloof and standoffish.

Your notes:_____

_____

_____

_____

#139 - ANGEL

<u>How have you been an angel to another person?</u>
- What is the best or nicest thing you have done for another person?

If it is hard for you to sing your own praises, describe a situation in which someone was an angel to you.

Your notes:_____

_____

_____

_____

#140 - IS A HOUSE A HOME

<u>Where is truly home to you?</u>
<u>What makes it home?</u>
- The people who live there
- The location
- The house itself

<u>Has your concept of home changed as you've aged?</u>
<u>Where is the place you felt was truly home?</u>
- A residence where you actually lived
- A place you saw while traveling
- A place you saw on television or the internet
- A place you've read or heard about
- The home where you grew up
- The home where you raised your family
- The home you live in now
- You have never lived in a place you felt was truly home

<u>Did you leave this home?</u>
<u>What happened to cause you to leave your home?</u>
- A required move to another city
- Divorce or other changes to the family unit
- Change in financial status
- Wanderlust
- Or?

Your notes:_____

_____

_____

_____

"Earthquakes"
by Joan Wallach
with gratitude to Cindy Reed

We were in our honeymoon phase ... a friendship had blossomed into love. Arthur, the New Yorker, had a Denver decade under his belt and was happily reacquainting me with my hometown, after 15 years away. Denver - still a cow town, land locked, high and dry. Denver - 300 days of sunshine, surrounding mountains' majesty, family and friends. Home.

We went to see Joan Baez at a venue now gone. We were transported by the music, brought back to the best in each other as we exited into the crisp autumn night. The next morning began with a shattering - though not unexpected - phone call. It was Arthur's brother Alan calling from San Francisco. Alan couldn't get out of bed. He needed an ambulance and needed Arthur to tell their parents why. Arthur knew Alan was living with AIDS, but Alan hadn't told anyone else. He had never come out to his parents. In crisis it was both easy to forgive a brother's cruel omissions and hell to make the unthinkable call.

We spoke of moving to San Francisco. We'd be there for Arthur's parents and could spend Alan's remaining time with him. San Francisco, a cultural and food mecca, was certainly alluring. Living together seemed a good step. Arthur's daughters would be close to their grandparents. We packed. We looked for a home. We researched schools. Arthur commuted every two weeks.

We visited that Halloween. It was ghoulish. Arthur's mother was disoriented and disconnected, her lung cancer having metastasized to her brain. And all too fast, Alan was declining. What could I do? I made applesauce, filling his home with the smells of cloves and cinnamon, but Alan declined the Cranes stationery with its eighth inch green trim. Weak, but with sensibilities intact, he proclaimed, "It's a little much."

Next trip - the surreal holiday visit. Christmas lights without snow and leaves still on the trees. Arthur and I shuttling from one hospital ward to another. Arthur's mother dying in one building, Alan struggling in the other. Rose died at the end of November. As we approached the synagogue, Alan fell. His weakness spoke to us in ways his mother's impersonal and sparsely attended funeral could not. Five weeks later, after morphine infused talk of a Mobius strip, Alan died. For his funeral we called in Denver family, and stayed up late into the night, weaving memories into a eulogy befitting this absent 48 year old man.

Finally, our move was complete. We settled in a rental home in the Berkeley Hills. We became a cobbled together family, with all its drama and angst. I was 33, the littlest of fish in the giant pond of San Francisco.

And yet. There were amazing inexpensive Chinese dinners, and long walks on Solano Avenue. There were bookstores aplenty, flowers in winter, wins for both daughters as they found their new people. There were stunning concerts, readings, sunsets at the ocean, morning buns and seedy baguettes ...

And yet again. There was the business. Theft, suicide, and vast debt preceded us. I lived to tell the tale of the burned out tax auditor who, on the cusp of retirement, looked at my boxes of documents, said something about my honest face, and gave us a reprieve.

What finally punctured our hope and resolve? Was it alarm company calls alerting us to business break-ins at 2:00 and 3:00 a.m.? Was it the collection calls from suppliers which penetrated Arthur's dreams and served as waking nightmares? Could it have been the 7.9 Richter scale earthquake that shook each of us to our core?

We stayed as long as we could. After the girls graduated from high school. After we married, exchanging rings symbolic of the Mobius strip. After the Oakland A's lifted us up. After Arthur's dad found a new companion. Only then could Arthur say what haunted him. He was lonely and overwhelmed. His losses compounded every day. He wanted out. It had taken seven years and aftershocks from losing Alan and Rose too numerous to count.

It was time to go home.

#141 - DRESS UP

<u>What costume would you wear to a costume party?</u>
<u>Have you ever worn this costume, or is it your fantasy costume?</u>
- If you have worn this costume, how did you feel being dressed as someone other than yourself?
- How did other people react to you? Did you like their reactions?

<u>If you never wore this costume, why not?</u>

Your notes:_____

_____

_____

_____

#142 - TIP

<u>What would you do for a tip?</u>
<u>What was the best tip you ever received?</u>
- For service, i.e. serving food in a restaurant
- Of an investment opportunity
- Or?

Your notes:_____

_____

_____

_____

#143 - TRAVEL

<u>Where have you traveled?</u>
- Where is the most exciting place you've visited?

<u>Who were your traveling companions?</u>
- Do you like to travel alone or with others?

<u>What is your favorite mode of transportation when you travel?</u>
- Plane
- Car
- Train
- Cruise ship or river boat
- Walking or hiking

- Bicycle
- Horse

What is the most daring or adventurous thing you have done while traveling?

Have you traveled to that one special place you've always wanted to see?

- What was it about this place that drew you to it?
- Did your experience live up to your expectations?

Have you ever been in danger or threatened while traveling?

Your notes:_____

_____

_____

_____

#144 - VACATION

Describe your vacations

- Favorite vacation
- Most disappointing vacation
- Vacation that was better than you expected

Describe your perfect vacation

- Where is it?
- What would you do when you got there?
- Who would you go with?
- Have you actually been on this vacation or is it a dream or fantasy?

Describe your worst or most disappointing day on a vacation

Your notes:_____

_____

_____

_____

SEVEN

We have a tendency to believe things are true simply because they are written down. You don't want a falsehood or misunderstanding to become accepted as true just because you put it down on paper and said it was so.

Use primary sources to verify information if they are available. Don't write that your brother was motivated to do something based on guesswork and your own biased observation if you are able to talk with him and verify information. If you need to verify facts with older friends and relatives, talk with them before it is too late to do so, and they are no longer available due to death or disability.

#145 - HAPPY AND GOOD

Go do something that makes you feel happy and write about it
Go do something that makes you feel good and write about it

Your notes:_____

_____

_____

_____

#146 - HAPPINESS

<u>What experience of yours made you the happiest?</u>
- Where do you anticipate happiness will strike next?

<u>If you had $20,000 to buy yourself some happiness, how would you spend it?</u>
- If you had $20,000 to buy happiness for someone else, how and on whom would you spend it?

Your notes:_____

_____

_____

_____

#147 - FAMILY FEUDS

<u>Is there a feud in your family?</u>
- What is your perspective of the feud?

<u>What caused it?</u>
- Estate or inheritance
- Misunderstandings about an issue or action
- Money
- Feeling you were not appreciated
- Unequal treatment of siblings by parents
- Jealousy
- Obligations not shared equally between family members
- Conflicts simmering since childhood

- It's not really a feud, you just have nothing in common
- Or?

<u>If there was a reconciliation, how did it come about?</u>
<u>If there was no reconciliation, do you believe the estrangement is permanent?</u>

- If the feud has not been resolved, what can you do to bring peace to the family?

Your notes:_____

_____

_____

_____

#148 - AMBITION

<u>Are you an ambitious person?</u>
<u>What was your ambition</u>

- As a child
- As a young adult
- In mid-career
- As a senior

<u>Did you achieve your ambitions?</u>
<u>How have your ambitions changed as you've aged?</u>

- Do you have any ambitions you still hope to achieve?

Your notes:_____

_____

_____

_____

#149 - BUTTONS

<u>What is the fastest way to make you angry?</u>

- What are your "hot buttons"?

Your notes:_____

_____

_____

_____

HELPFUL HINT #17 - NAME THOSE PEOPLE

If you include photos in your autobiography, be sure to caption them with the complete first and last names of all people pictured. People well known to you and your children may be unidentifiable strangers to future generations.

In addition, write the names of the people pictured and the date and place the picture was taken on the back of the photo itself.

#150 - PERFECT

<u>Describe the most perfect day you've had</u>
- Perfect holiday
- Perfect place visited
- Perfect day of school
- Perfect day with family
- Perfect celebration
- Wedding

- Birth of a child
- Graduation
- Significant milestone
- Perfect day being with another person or group of people
- Or?

Your notes:_____

_____

_____

_____

#151 - SPECIAL

To whom are you special?
- Spouse, parent, sibling, grandparent, other relative
- Job mentor
- Best friend

What makes you special to this person?
- Love
- Family relationships
- Friendship
- Shared interests or a "common cause"
- Shared history and background
- Or?

What does this special relationship mean to you?
How has this relationship been a factor in your decision-making?
- Advice you've been given
- Having a chance to talk things over
- Looking to this person as a role model

How has the nature of this relationship changed over time?

Your notes:_____

_____

_____

_____

❧

"The Red Shoes"
by Susan Fraizer

It was my fifth birthday. My grandfather, Carlo Aluffo Charles, was taking me shopping for a new outfit. That was something we didn't get very often. A lot of our clothes were second hand, which was alright because they were clean and presentable. But I knew I was going to a dress store for a new outfit. I was so excited! We went to a children's dress store in Alhambra, California. Grandpa and I went in and he asked for a saleslady to help us.

I remember walking among rows of beautiful dresses. They were fancy dresses with lace on the edge of beautiful sheer fabric. The underlining was silky fabric and so soft. I loved the pink dresses. That was the color I wanted. I picked the style I wanted and the saleslady brought everything in my size. I had a new slip, panties, white socks with lace trim, and a beautiful pale pink dress with little white dots on it, as soft as velvet. It was the most beautiful dress that was ever mine at the age of five.

Now it was time to pick out my new shoes. We went over to the shoe department and looked at all the shoes. It was almost overwhelming to know that I could have new shoes too. I spotted the exact pair I wanted. They were a beautiful red pair with a strap across the instep. I thought they were irresistible. I told the saleslady they were the shoes I wanted. She told me they were red and did not go with my new pink dress. I didn't understand it. I had the prettiest pink dress. Why not have the prettiest red shoes with it? The saleslady didn't want to give in. She said they just didn't go together. Grandpa stepped into the conversation. He told the saleslady that if his granddaughter wanted red shoes with her pink dress that was what she was going to have. The next thing I knew I was being fitted for my new red shoes. I was so happy.

Next my Grandpa did the most wonderful thing. I was all dressed up and ready to go. There were these long tables maybe three in a row. They were empty. He picked me up so I could stand on this "runway". He held my hand and walked me all the way down the tables singing, "Here she comes, Miss America," as loudly as he could. Everybody turned and watched as I finished my walk. He helped me down from the table and we walked out of the store.

What a glorious day it was. I have never forgotten the way he could make me feel so special.

#152 - CRIME

<u>Have you ever been the victim of a crime?</u>
- What happened?

<u>Was the criminal prosecuted?</u>
- Did you testify in court?

<u>Do you have any long term physical or emotional problems as a result of this crime?</u>

Your notes:_____

_____

_____

_____

#153 - CRIMINAL

<u>Have you ever broken the law?</u>
- What was your crime?

<u>What was the aftermath of your crime?</u>
- You got away with it
- You were arrested
- You were fined

- You were tried and convicted
- You were placed on probation
- You went to jail

Your notes:_____

_____

_____

_____

#154 - ARTIST

<u>How are you an artist?</u>

We are all artists in some way, so describe <u>how</u> you are an artist, not <u>if</u> you are an artist.

Your notes:_____

_____

_____

_____

#155 - ENCOURAGEMENT

<u>Who gave you the most encouragement?</u>
- What did this person say or do to encourage you?

Your notes:_____

_____

_____

_____

#156 - BULLY

<u>Describe a time when you were bullied</u>
<u>Describe a time when you bullied another person</u>

Your notes:_____

_____

_____

_____

#157 - SHOULDN'T

<u>Describe something you were told you shouldn't do, but went ahead and did anyway</u>
- What was the result of your having done this?
- Were you glad you did this thing, or did you later regret it?

Your notes:_____

_____

_____

_____

#158 - UNFAIR

<u>Write about a time when you were treated unfairly</u>
- As a child
- As an adult
- Now

Your notes:_____

_____

_____

_____

❧

═══

HELPFUL HINT #18 - READ

You learn to write by writing, but you also learn to write by reading. When you read a biography, autobiography, or memoir you especially enjoy, ask yourself what you liked about it. Try to incorporate the techniques you liked into your own writing.

I love to search my Kindle for out-of print memoirs and autobiographies. I've found some treasures that I would never have found without my Kindle. These are the stories of interesting people who led fascinating lives, but are now long forgotten. Don't read just popular contemporary memoirs or the autobiographies of famous people. Look also for the stories of people lost to the passage of time.

═══

❧

#159 - FASCINATING

<u>What fascinates you the most about yourself?</u>

Your notes:_____

_____

_____

_____

#160 - LOOK AT ME

<u>What do you do to attract attention?</u>
- How does being noticed influence the way you view yourself?

<u>Do you even want to attract attention?</u>

Your notes:_____

_____

_____

_____

#161 - YOUR DECADE

<u>What decade is yours?</u>
- What about your life in this decade defines you?
- How did your life in this decade influence you in subsequent years?
- What are your memories of this decade?

<u>Some suggestions:</u>
- The decade of your most vivid childhood memories
- The decade of young adulthood and your first taste of independence
- The decade in which you had your greatest financial success
- The decade in which you married and began your family
- The decade in which you had your greatest triumph
- The decade in which you had your greatest disappointment or challenge
- The decade in which you overcame adversity
- The decade in which you had a major change in status
- The decade in which you had a major shift in your philosophy of life
- The decade in which you are currently living

Your notes:_____

_____

_____

_____

#162 - BEST / WORST

═══

"It was the best of times, it was the worst of times ... "

- CHARLES DICKENS -

═══

❧

<u>What was?</u>

Your notes:_____

_____

_____

_____

#163 - FRIENDSHIP

<u>Who was your best friend as a child, as an adult, and now?</u>
- Are you still in contact with the best friend you had as a child?
- If your best friend is no longer part of your life, how has this impacted you?

<u>What qualities do you value most in a friend?</u>
- What qualities do you value most in the friends you have now?
- What qualities did you value most in the friends you had as a child?

<u>If you don't have a best friend, why not?</u>
- Don't want one
- Don't need one
- Haven't found one
- Don't like letting people get too close
- I have lots of friends, but none I consider the "best"

Your notes:_____

_____

_____

_____

#164 - PEOPLE FROM YOUR PAST

<u>"I wonder whatever happened to …"</u>
- Have you lost contract with someone who was once an important part of your life and wonder where they are now?

<u>Have you tried to track down this person?</u>

<u>If you got in contact, what happened?</u>
- Friendship renewed
- No longer any basis for a friendship, so the relationship was not renewed

Your notes:_____

_____

_____

_____

#165 - TRIBUTE

Write a tribute to a friend

Your notes:_____

_____

_____

_____

❧

"Thank You Carol"
by Maria C.

The second week of February was a tough time. February 14th I received an email from Anita, my former classmate, announcing the death of her husband Scott. The next day, another email from our school website came with the news that Dely's husband died after his bypass surgery. Then the most devastating news. Carol, our good friend, died on February 16th. I was not expecting this tragic news. We had just seen Carol in April of the previous year.

My college friends, Cecilia, Tina, Marissa, and I decided to go to Las Vegas for "special bonding days." Cecilia and I live in Los Angeles. Tina lives in Switzerland, and every year stays in California from November to March to escape the harsh Swiss winter. Marissa, a New Jersey resident, visits Los Angeles to spend time with her best friend, Tina. Cecilia and I hadn't seen Marissa since graduation, and were eager to see her again.

On our first day, while we were having dessert at our hotel's coffee shop, Tina kept checking her watch. She would often leave the group to take a personal call on her cell phone. Finally we found out the reason why Tina was so restless. She wanted to surprise us with the arrival of three more college friends.

Before we could finish dessert, we saw walking toward our table Boots, Becky, and Lina. Boots and Becky both live in Vegas, and Lina, a resident of Vancouver, flew in to join our mini reunion.

It was pure joy to see and reconnect with Boots, Becky, and Lina. It must have been close to twenty years since we last saw each other. We tried to recall how we looked back in college, and how we look now in our senior years. We unanimously agreed that we certainly looked gorgeous and didn't seem to have aged at all.

As we were planning our itinerary, Boots said we should take time to visit Carol. She also lived in Vegas, and the sad news was that Carol had terminal cancer. Boots would call to schedule our visit. Carol would let us know if she could see us, depending on how she felt that day. On our second day we received a call from Carol. She was feeling well and could see us.

We didn't know what to expect. After all, it's not every day you visit a terminally ill friend you haven't seen in decades. When we arrived at her place, Carol was standing by the entrance door. She'd lost a lot of weight, looked frail and gaunt, but still had that "tall and stately" bearing from our college years. Her once long wavy hair was cropped short and almost totally gray. Carol was a Math major and I was a Mass Communications major, so we hardly interacted in college, but we always had a friendly and warm relationship.

Carol warmly welcomed us to her cozy home. She had wine and cheese and a variety of finger foods prepared for us. Once we were seated, each one of us gave an update of our lives since graduation. When it was Carol's turn, she calmly told us she had advanced and terminal cancer. She talked openly about it, and even told us how many months the doctors gave her. Carol gave us all these details to answer the questions we might be hesitant to ask.

It was a bewitching afternoon. Each one of us brought up funny incidents in college, and we talked about other college friends and former professors. There was indeed wild, deafening, boisterous laughter from all of us. We completely transformed ourselves to our "young college girls" persona. All of us forgot the sad fact we were there to see our terminally ill friend Carol. For her part, Carol was just like one of us - loud, animated, and intense - especially when discussing political issues in Las Vegas. If you didn't know her condition, you would never guess she was someone in the last stages of life.

After almost three hours, we could sense Carol was getting tired. Our group bade her goodbye with tight hugs and embraces. The seven of us knew this might be the last time we'd see our dear friend Carol. There was sadness about her as she saw us off and waved goodbye. I'm sure it also crossed her mind this might be the last time for her to see us. As we drove off most of us looked one more time through the rear window just to catch a last glimpse of Carol, still standing by the door. We were all quiet and subdued as we drove back to our hotel.

The day we heard the sad news of Carol's death, Cecilia, Tina, and I exchanged long emails mourning the death of our dear friend. We all shared the same sentiment: that we were lucky and blessed to have seen Carol that April afternoon. The three of us treasured in our hearts that precious bonding time we spent with our dear friend Carol.

Carol was a courageous woman who didn't let cancer defeat her. She knew her days were numbered but this didn't stop her from living life to the fullest. That April afternoon our group learned a valuable lesson. Carol taught us that it is okay to accept your fate, be at peace with yourself, and most of all embrace what lies ahead. Carol was ready to let go of her earthly home and move on to her eternal home. She was one brave lady!

Rest in peace Carol, our dear friend. You will always be in our thoughts and prayers.

#166 - AGING BODY

<u>What things do you like most about your body as it is today?</u>
<u>What things do you miss that you can no longer do because of age, disability, or injury?</u>
- Changes in stamina
- Changes in strength
- Loss of hearing
- Weakening sight
- Or?

<u>How do you compensate for the losses you have experienced?</u>

Your notes:_____

_____

_____

_____

#167 - PERSONALITY

<u>What are the things you like most about your personality as it is today?</u>

Your notes:_____

_____

_____

_____

#168 - WORRY

<u>Are you a worrier?</u>
- What are the things you worry about?

Your notes:_____

_____

_____

_____

#169 - WILD

<u>What liberties would you like to take?</u>
- How would you go wild?

Your notes:_____

_____

_____

_____

EIGHT

HELPFUL HINT #19 - BEWARE OF YOUR POWER TO WOUND

After my father retired, he took writing classes at the local senior center. He had real talent, and left behind a legacy of stories dealing with his childhood, marriage, family, and career. In all those stories I, his only daughter, was mentioned just once, and then not even by name, but only as my brothers' sister. (My brothers were in many of the stories and always mentioned by name.) Even though my father is now deceased, this omission still hurts.

Remember you are writing your autobiography for others to read, and you do not want your tone to be hurtful, spiteful, or angry. You do not want to omit people - your children, your spouse, your parents, other family members - unless there is an estrangement and you have a valid reason for the omission. If there _is_ an estrangement, it is part of your story, and should be explained.

Check to see if you are wounding others by having a trusted but disinterested person read your story and tell you honestly how it sounds. This reader should <u>not</u> be a family member or some-one mentioned in your autobiography.

#170 - BREAKING UP

<u>Describe a time when you broke up with someone</u>
<u>Describe a time when someone broke up with you</u>

Your notes:_____

_____

_____

_____

#171 - THE AX

<u>As a supervisor, have you ever had to fire another person?</u>
- What did you say when you fired this person?

<u>How did firing this person make you feel?</u>
- Worried about the fired person's future, even though it had to be done
- Glad to see the person go
- Ambivalent - it was just part of your job

<u>Were there any unpleasant consequences as a result of firing this person?</u>
- Lawsuits
- Threats
- Complaints filed with government agencies or your employer
- Or?

Your notes:_____

_____

_____

_____

#172 - LOVEABLE

<u>Other than romantic love, how have you been loved?</u>
- By parents, siblings, friends

<u>How does it feel to be loved?</u>
- Are you loveable?

<u>Do you feel loved now?</u>

<u>Did you ever feel unloved by someone who was "supposed" to love you, i.e. a parent, child, or spouse?</u>
- How did that make you feel?

Your notes:_____

_____

_____

_____

#173 - JACKPOT!!

<u>How would you spend the money if you won millions in the lottery?</u>
- Would you invest your money to preserve your wealth or "blow it all" and live for the moment?

<u>Would you share your winnings?</u>
- With other people
- With charities or institutions

<u>What would you buy?</u>
- A new home
- Travel
- A fancy car
- Plastic surgery
- Or?

<u>What financial legacy would you leave if you were wealthy?</u>
- How would this legacy differ from the legacy you are currently able to leave?

Would you try to exercise control over others if you had a lot of money?
Would you exclude anyone or anything from your distribution of wealth?
* Why?
How would this jackpot change the way you live your life?
What would be bothersome about having a lot of money?
* Previously unknown relatives and friends asking for money
* Feeling unsafe and targeted by unscrupulous people
* People treating you differently or liking you only for your money

Your notes:_____

_____

_____

_____

#174 - WINNING

Describe a time when you won a prize
* What did you do to win this prize?
* What prize were you given?

Your notes:_____

_____

_____

_____

#175 - FEAR

When were you really afraid?

Your notes:_____

_____

_____

_____

❧

"Fear - A Roller Coaster Ride of Emotions"
by Lynda Barr

I was divorced from my first husband Dale for eight years by July 1985, and we had the rhythm down on which weekends our son and daughter would be staying with him and his wife Vivian, and who would do the picking up and dropping off each visit. My son Jeff had just turned 14 and his sister Robin was 12.

It was my turn to pick up the kids from Dale's home on Sunday, July 7th, and I came up to his front door and knocked. Dale answered but didn't say a word and looked very much in shock. I didn't see or hear the kids, and noticed Dale's brother and his wife were there and looked like they had been crying. Very quickly my fear mounted and I could feel my adrenalin pumping since I assumed something had happened to one or both of my kids. I immediately imagined them killed in some horrible accident and that it must have just happened. I could barely breathe and felt very panicky and demanded that he tell me what happened. What he said was, "My mom was murdered by the Night Stalker".

To this day I still feel so much guilt in the split-second of immediate relief I felt that my kids were alive. Then, in the next few seconds my emotions returned to a horrified feeling. I also felt extreme shame for feeling relief. As I entered his home, I asked Dale how he knew it was the Night Stalker who killed his mom. He told me the police had come and let him know she had been murdered that morning at 2:30 a.m., and gave him the reasons why they knew it was Richard Ramirez. My kids came out from one of the other rooms, and I saw they were very upset and crying. I tried to console them, but knew nothing would ever bring back their only living Grandma.

The next few weeks continued to be extremely tense since the Night Stalker was still on the loose and still killing. When Richard Ramirez saw his photo in the newspapers on August 31, 1985, he panicked and began running through an East LA neighborhood. Within minutes, he was recognized and caught by angry residents and was being kicked and beaten with a tire iron. Unfortunately the police arrived too soon and he was arrested and taken away.

Richard Ramirez, who was then 25 years old, had begun terrorizing southern California in late 1984. He murdered thirteen people and brutalized two dozen more during the next year. Three years later his trial began, and Dale and other family members attended as many of the court proceedings as they could. What made the horror of those days continue for surviving victims and their families was the way Richard Ramirez was so callously arrogant during the court proceedings, and how he laughed as the details of each murder were read in court. He was eventually convicted of first degree murder in all cases, plus thirty more felonies, and sentenced to death.

Richard Ramirez died at Marin General Hospital in Greenbrae, California on June 7, 2007 at the age of 53. He died from complications related to B-cell lymphoma while awaiting execution on California's Death Row at San Quentin. News of his death traveled fast, and finally gave some long awaited closure to many people. The date of his death was one day after my son Jeff's 35th birthday, and was probably his best gift that year.

#176 - FEARFUL

<u>What did you not do because you were afraid?</u>
<u>Why were you afraid?</u>
- Health issues
- Money issues
- Lack of confidence in your abilities
- Unwilling to take a risk

- Fear of physical harm
- Phobias, i.e. fear of heights, fear of speaking in public
- Feelings of danger or threat
- Or?

<u>Were you able to overcome your fear?</u>

- Did you learn any lessons from your inaction due to fear that changed the way you lead your life?

Your notes:_____

_____

_____

_____

#177 - REGRET (1)

<u>What are the "should haves" in your life?</u>

- When you were young
- At mid-life
- Now

<u>What is your biggest regret?</u>

Your notes:_____

_____

_____

_____

#178 - REGRET (2)

"This above all: to thy own self be true."

- WILLIAM SHAKESPEARE -

<u>Did you ever ignore that little voice inside you, and instead do something that didn't feel quite right?</u>

- Wrong job
- Wrong vacation
- Wrong spouse
- Wrong lover
- Wrong house
- Or?

<u>What was the result?</u>

Your notes:_____

_____

_____

_____

#179 - WORTH

<u>Was it really worth it?</u>

Your notes:_____

_____

_____

_____

#180 - THE FIRST TIME

<u>Write about the first time you:</u>
- Kissed someone in a romantic way
- Had a "crush"
- Drove a car
- Bought a car
- Traveled to a foreign country
- Earned a paycheck
- Fell in love
- Had sex
- Gave a speech
- Rode a bike
- Flew in an airplane
- Took a <u>real</u> vacation
- Shot a gun
- Won a prize
- Earned an "A"
- Flunked a class
- Forgot your lines
- Went to a concert
- Ate at a "fancy" restaurant
- Voted in an election
- Taught a new skill
- Learned a new skill

- Wore formal clothing
- Drank too much
- Opened a bank account
- Got a credit card

Approach this exercise in any way that works for you. You may choose to write a few sentences on many topics, or several pages on just one topic.

Your notes:_____

_____

_____

_____

※

_____

HELPFUL HINT #20 - SHOW DON'T JUST TELL

Engage your readers so they want to experience your life with you. What was it like to be you at that moment in time? Don't just describe; help your reader re-live the experience with you. When you were living through an event, you didn't know what would happen. You didn't know if you'd get that job, get accepted to that school, survive that surgery, or accept that proposal. We don't know what will eventually happen as we live our daily lives. Try to bring that sense of anticipation and the unknown to your story.

- Use all your senses to tell your story. Describe not only what you saw, but also what you felt, smelled, heard, and tasted. Set the scene: the smell of a holiday, the taste of that first kiss, the feel of a beloved pet's head under your hand.
- Don't stand apart from what you are writing and from your experiences. Bring emotion into your story to make it come alive.

- Take ownership of what you write. Don't use passive language that distances you from your story. Write, "I know," rather than "It is known," or "I believe," rather than "It is generally believed."

Above all else, WRITE FROM YOUR HEART!

#181 - YOUR SENSES

Describe your favorite (or least favorite) smell, sight, touch, taste or sound
- Why it is your favorite (or least favorite)

When you experience this sense, what is your reaction?
- What does it make you do?
- How does it make you feel?
- What does it mean to you?
- What memories does it awaken?
- In what part of your body do you sense it?

How have your senses changed as you've aged?
- Is there a sense you never had, lost, or no longer have full use of?
- How does not having this sense impact you?

Are you more or less sensitive to certain things - noises too loud, lights too dim, little tiny print where it was once large enough - than you used to be?

Your notes:_____

_____

_____

_____

"Redondo"
by C.H.B.

The Helms Bakery truck. The distinctive sound of its whistle - whoo, whoo. The delicious-ness when the drawer of donuts was pulled open and out wafted that sweet yeasty sugary golden smell. Even after all these years I can still see the driver swing open the rear doors of his truck and pull out that polished wooden drawer full of donuts. And I still smell it - that perfect fat shiny glazed donut.

My brothers and I weren't allowed to buy donuts from the Helms man. Mom always said that if we were hungry after school we could have a piece of fruit. But Nancy, who lived at the bottom of the hill, bought a donut every day - probably because she was so skinny. Nancy's mother had a VW van, and Nancy, Lynda, Judy, and I would sit in the van when it was parked in Nancy's driveway and pretend to be the Beatles on tour. I was Ringo, Nancy was George, Lynda was John, and Judy was Paul.

Playing with Judy was always the best fun because she had such an incredible imagination. Our Barbies had the most amazing adventures. Sometimes they were at a Swiss boarding school, and sometimes they owned a horse ranch, and sometimes they were spies, intriguing with James Bond and Jim Phelps. We may have been at Judy's house playing Monopoly, but in our minds we were riding the Orient Express, negotiating with the mysterious strangers who shared our compartment. I can still feel the excitement of the stories Judy wove around a simple game of Monopoly we played in her living room one rainy Redondo night.

#182 - GRIEF

<u>Things have happened in your life that caused you grief</u>
- Death of family and friends
- Job loss
- Substance abuse issues

- Loss of youth
- Doubt
- Death of a pet
- Divorce or loss of a relationship
- Moving
- Financial setbacks
- Loss due to natural disaster, i.e. earthquake, tornado, fire, flood, drought
- Health problems
- War

Describe your feelings

- Anger
- Sadness
- Loss
- Betrayal
- Forgotten
- Ignored
- Loneliness
- Despair
- Loss of faith
- Calm
- Resignation and acceptance
- Renewed faith
- Love
- It's just not fair
- Or?

Did family or friends ignore or try to brush aside your feelings by not talking about your grief?

- How did that make you feel?

Do you need to forgive anyone or anything in order to deal with your grief?

- What will you do to forgive?

Your notes:_____

_____

_____

_____

#183 - MAGIC (1)

Describe a "magical moment"

Your notes:_____

_____

_____

_____

#184 - MAGIC (2)

About what do you think magically?

Your notes:_____

_____

_____

_____

#185 - TREASURED THINGS

In the book *Little Women*, the narrator Jo, now an adult, writes about four chests filled by the sisters Meg, Amy, Beth, and Jo herself when they were children. The chests, now "Dim with dust, and worn by time," are filled with the treasured possessions of the little girls.

Find a treasure chest of your own to fill with memories. It could be a box you buy or something you make. Then write about the things you put into it.

<u>What did you put in your treasure chest?</u>
- Why are these things important to you?
- What memories does each thing represent?
- Are they happy or sad memories?
- With whom did you make these memories?

<u>Out of all the things you own, why did you choose these particular items to put in your chest?</u>
- What makes these things important in telling the story of your life?

Your notes:_____

_____

_____

_____

#186 - HAVING A GOOD TIME

<u>What is the best time you ever had?</u>
- Where were you?
- What happened that was so enjoyable?
- Who was with you?

<u>What memory still makes you smile when you think about it?</u>

Your notes:_____

_____

_____

_____

#187 - PROUD

<u>What is your proudest accomplishment?</u>
- Family and children
- Career or profession
- Achievements in education or sports
- Conquering a personal challenge, i.e. acquiring patience, overcoming shyness, mending broken relationships
- Overcoming illness or injury
- A time you behaved kindly or honorably
- Or?

Your notes:_____

_____

_____

_____

NINE

HELPFUL HINT #21 - IT'S NOT A HISTORY LESSON

Don't use your memoir to display your knowledge of historical events. No one likes a know-it-all, so don't lecture. Insert a few facts to set the scene, but don't go overboard. Stating that your family moved to the farm after your father lost his job during the Great Depression is enough. You do not need to overwhelm your readers with pages of dispassionate economic theory and history.

To help establish context do some research and find out what happened during the time about which you are writing. But remember, this is your story, so use only a few sentences to set the scene. You are writing the story of your life, not a history textbook!

#188 - THEN AND NOW

<u>How was your childhood different from the way children grow up now?</u>
<u>What things were in use when you were growing up that are now out of use or obsolete?</u>
- Cars with manual transmissions
- Mimeograph machines
- Typewriters
- And?

What things are in use now that you did not have when you were growing up?
- Cell phones
- Computers
- DVDs
- And?

What things from your childhood do you think would be useful to children growing up today?
- Physical objects
- Concepts and values

Your notes:_____

_____

_____

_____

#189 - ANIMALS (1)

Write about your memory of an animal
- Favorite pet
- An animal that scared you
- A friend's pet
- A sighting or encounter with a wild animal
- A fictional animal you may have cried over or wished you owned
  - Ginger in *Black Beauty*
  - Charlotte in *Charlotte's Web*
  - Misty in *Misty of Chincoteague*
  - Lassie
- An animal you just don't like

What do you like about animals?
What do you dislike about animals?
Sometimes I like animals better than
- Friends
- Relatives

- Spouse
- Co-workers
- People in general

Are you afraid of any animals?
- An individual animal
- A particular breed, i.e. pit bulls
- A particular species, i.e. all cats
- Wild animals

Your notes:_____

_____

_____

_____

#190 - ANIMALS (2)

Are you a "dog person" or a "cat person"?

Your notes:_____

_____

_____

_____

#191 - WHO'S THAT?

Have you ever been on a blind date?
How did it work out?
- Where did you go?
- What did you do?

What did you talk about?
- Did you have anything in common?

Did a romance or friendship develop, or was it just a one-time meeting?

Your notes:_____

_____

_____

_____

#192 - SCARY

"The passage that had to be negotiated was interminably long and lit only by an oil lamp at its far end. This was an awful place, for under a marble slab in its dim recesses, a stuffed crocodile reposed. In the daytime the crocodile PRETENDED to be very dead, but everyone knew that as soon as it grew dark, the crocodile came to life, and padded about the passage on its scaly paws seeking for its prey, with its great cruel jaws snapping, its fierce teeth gleaming, and its horny tail lashing savagely from side to side. It was also common knowledge that the favorite article of diet of crocodiles was a little boy with bare legs in a white suit."

- FREDERICK SPENCER HAMILTON -

<u>What scared you when you were a child?</u>
- The dark
- Thunder and lightening
- Water or drowning
- Dogs
- Wild animals
- Bugs or spiders

- The neighborhood "haunted" house
- Heights
- Locked rooms
- The "boogie man"
- Bad dreams
- The scary place your parents told you not to go
- Earthquakes, floods, or other natural disasters
- War or "the bomb"
- Being physically hurt
- Violence and guns
- Ghosts
- Aliens, trolls, monsters, or gnomes
- Something under your bed
- Strangers

How did you get the idea that this thing was scary?

- Something a parent or sibling said to you
- Something a friend told you or that "everyone" knew
- It was dark or hard to see clearly
- You misunderstood something said to you

How did you deal with your fear?

- Run away
- Close your eyes
- Hold your breath
- Make a wish
- Talk to a family member
- Sleep with your parents
- Say a prayer
- Try to ignore it
- Or?

How did you overcome your fear?

Your notes:_____

_____

_____

_____

#193 - PETS

<u>What were your family pets?</u>
- As a child
- As an adult
- Now

<u>Did you have one pet that was extra special to you?</u>
- Why was this one pet more special to you than your other pets?

<u>Do you have a pet no longer with you that you still miss?</u>

Your notes:_____

_____

_____

_____

❧

_____
_____

"Taffy"
by Sallie Ringle

It was Christmas Eve 1953, and the family was sitting at the dining table. I heard jingle bells. What's that? The bells were really loud and right outside our house. There was a "Ho Ho Ho," and a knock at the door. Mom asked me to answer it. I opened the door and there was Santa. Tucked under his arm was a little brown and white puppy with floppy ears and a huge red bow. There was a tag on the bow and it read "Sallie & Steve". My brother Steve came running up and so did my cousins. We all crowded around

Santa. He asked if we thought we were old enough to take care of a puppy. Of course we said YES! That night reinstated my belief in Santa Claus. At nine I thought I was too big to believe in him. I was wrong. Santa had come and brought me a puppy. He brought her on Christmas Eve because he was afraid that riding in his sleigh would be too hard for a little puppy and she might get cold.

Being the older sister, I latched on to the dog first. She was so soft and kissed me right away all over my face. Dad had made a place where we were to keep the puppy until she was housebroken. Mom said we needed to give her a name. Everyone had an idea. Mom suggested we call her Taffy because her coat was the color of salt water taffy with white. So we agreed - Taffy it would be.

Taffy became my confidant over the years. I taught her to walk and "heel", first on a leash but in time she was so good walking I could take her on long walks without the leash and she would never leave my side. She would always come bounding home when we called or Dad whistled for her. As I got to be 12 to 14 years old I would take Taffy on walks to secluded places and talk to her. Sometimes I would cry because I was an emotional teen and needed someone to talk to. Taffy was the best friend I had. I continued to pay lots of attention to Taffy, my beloved dog, even in my high school years.

I have had many dogs over the years but Taffy was always my favorite. She was my best friend when I needed one. I left home when I was 18 and my brother left a couple of years after that. Mom and Dad decided to sell the family home and move into a condo. Steve was off at college, I had moved to northern California, and Mom and Dad decided they didn't want to take Taffy to live in the condo. They never consulted my brother or me. They just took her to the animal shelter to be adopted. Who would adopt a 12 year old dog? I have always been sure that the shelter put her down. For years I resented my parents for doing that to Taffy. She deserved to be loved to the end. I will always love her.

#194 - LET ME HELP

<u>Describe any volunteer work you do</u>
<u>What are the areas of interest of your volunteer work?</u>

- School or education related activities
- Religious activities
- Scouting
- Rotary, Junior League, or other community assistance organizations
- Environmental or conservation groups
- Fraternal organizations such as Masons or Elks
- Healthcare or disease prevention
- Political activism
- Children
- Animals
- Athletics

Your notes:_____

_____

_____

_____

#195 - THANKS

Write a thank you note to something or someone, but **not** a person you know
Here are some suggestions:
- Electronics. i.e. computer, Kindle, telephone, TV
- A piece of furniture
- A certain food
- A holiday or other celebration
- Shoes or an article of clothing
- Car, plane, train, bike
- A favorite book or fictional character
- A favorite author or performer
- A favorite form of entertainment
- Nature, forests, ocean, mountains, plants, or flowers
- One of your body parts, character traits, or physical traits

- An enjoyable sensory experience
- A certain city, state, or country
- Animals (pets or in nature)
- Modern appliances, i.e. air conditioner, refrigerator, stove, microwave
- Indoor plumbing
- Your school or education
- Your special talents or skills
- Humor and laughter
- Religious beliefs and traditions
- Constitutional rights
- Where you live
- Retirement

This is not meant to be a list of things for which you are grateful, so try not to write things like, "I am thankful for …" Instead, write a "thank you" note to something important in your life. For example, if you are a book lover you might write, "Dear Kindle: Thank you for showing me a whole new world with even more books. I love you so much."

Your notes:_____

_____

_____

_____

HELPFUL HINT #22 - YOU'RE NOT ALWAYS A HERO

You may be tempted to construct your story so you are always the hero and always right. If you want to tell your true story, try to tell the entire truth. No one is always heroic, and no one always makes the right decision.

Be conscious of portraying yourself accurately. Your reader needs to trust that you are telling the truth. No one's life is perfect, and no one lives their life without making mistakes and doing some embarrassing things. You do not have to shamelessly strip yourself naked, and too many uncensored revelations could make your readers uncomfortable. But if you are not accurate in your self-portrayal people will have doubts, and may see you and your story as works of fiction.

#196 - SHIPWRECK

<u>If you were shipwrecked on a deserted island, what would you take with you?</u>
- Electronic devices
- Books
- Music and movies
- Writing materials
- Art and drawing materials
- Another person
- A companion animal
- A boat
- Or?

<u>How long could you be on a deserted island before you'd want to return to civilization?</u>
- Or would you rather stay on your island?

Try not to be limited by logic. Assume that you have enough food, water, clothing, sun screen and shelter for your comfort. Do not worry about bringing practical things to your island. This is an exercise in fantasy. Release your imagination and write!

Your notes:_____

_____

_____

_____

#197 - WEIRD

<u>Describe the most outlandish, weird, or bizarre thing that has happened to you</u>

Your notes:_____

_____

_____

_____

#198 - THINKING

<u>What have you been thinking about lately?</u>
- Where does your mind go when it wanders?

Your notes:_____

_____

_____

_____

#199 - LAZY

"I'm lazy. But it's the lazy people who invented the wheel and the bicycle because they didn't like walking or carrying things."

- Lech Walesa -

<u>Are you lazy?</u>
- When are you lazy?
- How do you overcome your laziness and accomplish the things you need to do?

Your notes:_____

_____

_____

_____

#200 - PAIN

<u>I didn't think I'll ever get over this</u>
- Death of a loved one
- A missed opportunity
- Illness
- Sad memories from childhood
- Lost love
- An abandonment
- Or?

<u>But you're still here and you survived. How did you learn to live with your pain?</u>

Your notes:_____

_____

_____

_____

#201 - ATTACK

<u>Have you ever been attacked?</u>

Describe what happened
- A physical attack such as an assault
- An attack on your character or integrity

How did you react to being attacked?

How was the issue resolved?
- Arrest of the attacker
- Confrontation with the attacker
- Apology from the attacker
- Or?

Your notes:_____

_____

_____

_____

#202 - CALL BACK

Did your failure to return a call or answer a letter or email ever change your life?
- Was the change positive or negative?
- What happened?

Your notes:_____

_____

_____

_____

#203 - DID IT

I didn't think I could do it, but I did

Your notes:_____

_____

_____

_____

HELPFUL HINT #23 - EXPLAIN YOURSELF

In an ancient Buddhist story, a group of blind men is asked to describe an elephant by feeling different parts of its body. One man feels the leg and says the elephant looks like a pillar. One man feels the tail and says the elephant looks like a rope, and one man feels the tusk and says the elephant looks like a pipe.

Like the men in this story, we each look at things from our own perspective, making it easy to misjudge the actions and motivations of others. Do not assume that people understand all of your reasons for doing things.

Explain yourself. Tell your readers who you are. Use words to paint the picture you want your readers to have of you. You do not want others to have false ideas about you based on their own misperceptions and misunderstandings.

#204 - FORWARD

<u>What keeps you looking forward with hope and anticipation?</u>
- Retirement
- Travel
- New relationships

- New moves
- Spending more time with family and friends
- New career opportunities
- And?

<u>What things keep you from looking forward with hope and anticipation?</u>
- Money worries
- Concerns about physical and mental health
- Loneliness
- End of life issues
- Unresolved issues and estrangements
- Or?

Your notes:_____

_____

_____

_____

#205 - HEART

Try holding your heart in your hand. Make a small stuffed handmade heart, a paper heart, a felt heart, a heart you create from craft materials, or a rock that looks like a heart, and then decorate it.

<u>Write about your heart</u>
- Feeling heart
- Healing heart
- Compassionate heart
- Loving heart
- Sacred heart
- Grieving heart
- Broken heart
- Parental heart
- Patient heart

- Overflowing heart
- Giving heart

How did it feel to take your heart in your hand?

Your notes:_____

_____

_____

_____

#206 - KINDNESS

Describe a random act of kindness
- Something you did for someone else
- Something someone did for you
- An unexpected kindness from a casual acquaintance or stranger

Your notes:_____

_____

_____

_____

"Cancer and Kindness"
by Ann Hamer

In November 1998, after having a mammogram, ultrasound, and excisional biopsy, I was diagnosed with breast cancer. I was a student then and had very little money and no health insurance. All the testing to determine I had cancer was paid for by the state of California through a special breast cancer testing initiative, but after I was diagnosed, my choice seemed to be either death or debt. It took two months and many phone calls to find a way to fund my treatment. Susan G. Koman and the American Cancer Society both told me they funded only research, not treatment, and did not know where I could get help. Other calls to other places were equally unhelpful. I finally talked to the right person at the office of the California breast cancer initiative - the office that had funded the original testing - and got the OK to begin treatment. I was scheduled to have a mastectomy in February 1999.

At the time, I was renting the upstairs of Marsha's house while she lived downstairs. Marsha had become a good friend, and although she had plans to go to Monterey the weekend before my mastectomy, she offered to stay home and provide encouragement and many glasses of wine prior to Monday's surgery. I told her to go ahead with her plans because my friend Tracy had promised to come to Upland and spend the weekend with me.

On Friday, just a few hours before Tracy was due to arrive, she phoned and said she was not coming. She wanted to work that weekend, her cat was sick, and her boyfriend's parents (who did not speak English) were in town. I told her I was hurt. She had made me a promise, I had relied on her promise, and Marsha had gone off to Monterey. I told Tracy she could work any time, to tell her boyfriend to take care of the cat, and to ask him to make her excuses to his parents. In response, Tracy absolutely BLASTED me. She said she was a good friend, and a good girlfriend, and a good daughter, and a good sister, and a good employee (and presumably a good cat owner, although she did not say so.) I just had to understand. And then she hung up.

I started crying. I was going to be mutilated in less than three days, Tracy had backed out on me, and Marsha had gone ahead with her weekend plans - because I said it was OK to do so. Mom would have come - she and Dad were planning to come for the surgery anyway - but even though I love Mom a lot, sometimes she is just way too motherly. I wanted to make jokes and laugh and be silly and eat lots of sugar. I wanted a friend.

I had a friend from school, Patty, who I thought I might be able to ask. I was hesitant because she was married and worked two part-time jobs, so her weekends were always busy. She knew about my cancer, and at my "Say good-bye to Ann's left breast" party, she had written and sung two songs for me, one of which included the immortal line, "Now that you're a one-breasted woman, you'll have to find a one-handed man."

I called Patty. I apologized. I said I knew it was last minute, and I was sorry to ask, but could she, would she, please come to Upland and spend some time with me. She responded with absolutely no hesitation and said, "I'll be there. I'll be there for as long as you need me to be there." And she was. And it meant everything to me - because she surprised me with her kindness, because she did not hesitate, and because she just came.

Patty and I were school friends - we had classes together, hung out on campus, ate out a few times with other friends, had fun together. Until this happened, I would have considered her a good friend, but not one of my closest friends. But she stepped up for me, and I'll never forget it.

It has been many years since my mastectomy. I am cancer-free. Patty and I lost touch after she graduated, and I have not seen her for a long time. Tracy <u>did</u> call my mom after my surgery to ask how I was doing. I spoke with her when I got home from the hospital, and told her I was fine. Later I wrote Tracy telling her how hurt I had been, that I wanted to stay friends, but things needed to change. I was tired of arranging our get-togethers and driving long distances to see her, only to have her give me just an hour of her time because she had to go to the gym or hit a bucket of golf balls or knit an afghan. I showed the letter to Marsha. She said it was a good letter, not unkind, just stating what I needed. Marsha also said I should not be surprised if Tracy did not reply. She was right - I never heard from Tracy again.

I now live with my mom, and Marsha and I are still good friends.

#207 - GENEROSITY

<u>Who has surprised you with his or her generosity?</u>
- How did this act of generosity make you feel?

Your notes:_____

_____

_____

_____

#208 - RISE

How did you rise to the occasion?

Your notes:_____

_____

_____

_____

#209 - WRONG

Describe a time when you were wrong

Your notes:_____

_____

_____

_____

#210 - BECAUSE OF YOU

What exists because you are here?

Your notes:_____

_____

_____

_____

#211 - VANITY

<u>What have you done to satisfy your vanity?</u>
- Plastic surgery
- Spa treatments
- Crash diets
- Taking part in sports or activities generally done by younger people

<u>How did it make you feel to do these things?</u>
- Glad - I feel better because I look better
- I wasted my time and money

Your notes:_____

_____

_____

_____

TEN

If you have kept journals throughout your life, you may think that all you have to do to create your memoir is transcribe your journals onto your computer. But journals are not memoirs. Journals can be introspective, critical, and maybe even bitchy and self-absorbed. You want your readers to be interested in your life story, not think you are a whiny cry-baby. Too much introspection is boring and will never tell your readers your story.

Use your journals to remember where you were, what you were doing, and how you felt at certain times of your life. You may be tempted to use your journals to re-examine your mental state, but try to find a place other than your memoir for psychological musings. Put them in your second book!!

#212 - SURVIVOR

<u>Do you have any survivor guilt?</u>
- You survived when others didn't
- Your injuries were less severe than those of other survivors

<u>How have you dealt with your survivor guilt?</u>
- Learned to accept it

- Developed gratitude for your survival
- Tried to forget what happened
- Tried to convince yourself that things were a lot worse for you than they actually were in order to feel something in common with other survivors
- Or?

Your notes:_____

_____

_____

_____

#213 - BEFORE

<u>What are the things you want to do before you die?</u>
- A physical challenge, i.e. climb a mountain, run a marathon
- Travel to a certain place
- Something you are afraid of doing, i.e. ride a horse, parachute, speak in public
- Something you wish you had done when you were younger
- Mend relationships
- Get in touch with someone from your past
- Tell someone you love them
- Or?

Your notes:_____

_____

_____

_____

#214 - AGING

<u>Now that you are older, what things do you think you may have done for the last time?</u>
- Wearing pantyhose, Spanx, and heels

- Wearing a suit
- Writing a paper or taking a test
- Taking extended trips
- Having sex
- Owning a pet
- Being in love or in a relationship
- Participating in a sport you once enjoyed
- Or?

<u>Why do you no longer do these things?</u>
- "I'm retired and I don't have to"
- Mobility or strength issues
- Fear of being hurt or injured
- Loss of interest in things you used to do
- "I'm too old; that stuff is just for kids"

<u>Do you miss doing these things?</u>
- What new interests have you developed now that you no longer do these things?

<u>"What do you mean I'm too old - I still do these things!!"</u>

Your notes:_____

_____

_____

_____

❧

"My Louie"
by Rosemary Ventura

My husband Louie always loved golf from the time he was a teenager. He caddied for golfers at Split Rock Golf Course in Pelham, New York, close to the Bronx where he lived. He became a good player himself, good enough that the golf pro at Split Rock took him under his wing and was his mentor. However,

Louie's father would have none of it. He said that Louie couldn't be playing golf - "that's a game." He had to get a job and go to work. That's the way it was back then. There was no money to spend on golf lessons. He needed to bring in a salary and help the family, and he did. Louie's father was a truck driver for H.J. Korten Trucking, and he got Louie a job loading the trucks. He was 18 years old. It wasn't too long before Louie became a truck driver himself and that was the end of his golfing career until he retired and devoted most of his time to golf.

After Louie retired, he went to school to learn to be a golf instructor, and eventually taught juniors and adults how to play. He taught for the cities of Rancho Cucamonga, Upland, and San Bernardino. Louie was a pretty good player and played in many tournaments. He loved golf so much - both teaching and playing. He even repaired golf clubs. It broke his heart and mine when, because of his back surgeries, he couldn't play anymore. He marshaled at Upland Hills Golf Course and he enjoyed that every much. He loved volunteering, first with the Upland Police Department, and then with the San Bernardino County Sheriff's Department. In spite of all the pain, he always wanted to be involved in something.

#215 - RULES FOR LIFE

As an adult, you may have things you wish you had done differently or known "back then". Your successes inspire, and your failures provide lessons and warnings. This is your opportunity to share your "Rules for Life". These are your secrets for living an effective life.

<u>What are your Rules for Life?</u>
<u>What advice would you offer to others?</u>
- Pitfalls to avoid
- Where to find contentment, success, and happiness
- How to deal with the inevitable disappointments and challenges of life
- How to correct your mistakes and move forward

<u>What do you wish you hadn't done or had done more often?</u>
<u>How can you be true to yourself and listen to your heart?</u>

Your notes:_____

_____

_____

_____

#216 - GROWING INTO

<u>What are ten reasons you love being over 50?</u>
- What is the best thing about growing older?

<u>Here are some suggestions</u>
- Wisdom comes with maturity
- Less pressure and competition
- More leisure time
- Retirement
- A more relaxed frame of mind
- Self-acceptance
- Gaining perspective
- More time to spend with family and friends
- Attaining goals
- Or?

<u>If you are not yet over 50, list at least 10 reasons you love being your current age</u>

Your notes:_____

_____

_____

_____

#217 - MENDING

<u>Do you have fences to mend or things to say in order to make peace with yourself or others?</u>
- What could you say or do to mend those fences?

Your notes:_____

_____

_____

_____

#218 - PLEASES

<u>What pleases you the most about your life?</u>

Your notes:_____

_____

_____

_____

❧

HELPFUL HINT #25 - USE CONTEMPORARY LANGUAGE

Make your story real to your readers by using words and phrases popular during the time about which you are writing.

Pat Beauchamp served with the First Aid Nursing Yeomanry in France and Belgium during the First World War. She was from the British upper class, and knew very little about practical things. This excerpt from her story, published in 1919, effectively captures the time, place, and personality of the writer.

"Before Bridget left, she explained how I was to light the Primus stove … When the time came, I put the mentholated in the little cup at the top, lit it, and then pumped with a will. The result was a terrific roar and a sheet of flame reaching almost to the roof! Never having seen one in action before, I thought it was

possible they always behaved like that at first and that the conflagration would subside in a few moments. I watched it doubtfully, arms akimbo. Bridget entered just then, and determined not to appear flustered, in as cool a voice as possible I said, "Is that all right old thing?" She put down her parcels and, without a word, seized the stove by one of its legs and threw it on a sand heap outside! Of course the stove had gone out ... and I felt I was not the brightest jewel I might have been."

- Pat Beauchamp Washington –

#219 - PERSPECTIVES (1)

How have your perspectives about your own past actions and decisions changed as you've aged?

Your notes:_____

_____

_____

_____

#220 - PERSPECTIVES (2)

How do you think differently about things now that you are older?
- Politics
- Religion
- Your parents and family
- And?

Your notes:_____

_____

_____

_____

#221 - SUDDEN

<u>Write about something that changed your life overnight (suddenly and unexpectedly)</u>
- Unexpected award or honor
- Love at first sight
- Accident
- Unexpected death
- Unanticipated loss
- Unexpected inheritance
- A windfall
- Or?

Your notes:_____

_____

_____

_____

#222 - OLD FOLKS

<u>Who was the oldest member of your family when you were a child?</u>
<u>What was the status of this person in your family?</u>
- Revered and respected for wisdom gained from a long life
- Discounted and forgotten as someone too old to matter

<u>What is the story of this person?</u>
- Name
- Birth date and birth place
- When and where this person died and is buried

<u>What stories did this person tell you about their youth and young adulthood?</u>
<u>What are your memories of this person?</u>
- Were there any special things just the two of you did together?

Your notes:_____

_____

_____

_____

❧

"Da"
by Christine Jeston

The oldest member of my family when I was growing up was my mother's father. George Boreham McLeod was born in Edinburgh, Scotland in 1879. We called him Da. His father, Robert McLeod, was an interior decorator who mixed his own paints and was well known in Edinburgh and Glasgow for his colors. His family was not very well off due to his excessive drinking. I suppose that had an influence on Da's life as he never drank alcohol. He was also a pacifist and a socialist when he grew up.

When Da was a young boy he learned to box, and one day some bullies jumped him. A postman saw Da had the upper hand, so he held him down, and the other boys kicked him so badly that his woolen sock became embedded in one of his legs. He was afraid to tell his parents, and so his leg never healed properly. He suffered all his life because of it. Doctors wanted to amputate Da's leg, but my grandma had heard of a German doctor in Sydney and decided to take Da to see him. The doctor saved his leg by putting Fuller's Earth on it. It was something Da did every day of his life, and then wrapped clean bandages around the leg. I was horrified when I spied his leg one day as it looked to me like very thin almost opaque skin stretched over black and blue flesh and bone. The image has never left me.

The house at 13 Ethel Street Vaucluse where Ma and Da lived had a glasshouse out the back. It was full of boxes of tiny colored glass which threw off many colors and wonderful patterns when the sun shone through them. It was so magical and I just loved that little house. Sometimes Da would forage around in there for hours moving the glass around not saying anything, but I would be at his heels watching him. He had the largest lead light business in Sydney during the 1920s and 1930s. They were very well off and lived in a big house. He made beautiful stained glass windows, doors, and chandeliers that hung in some very prominent homes and famous buildings. Da lost the business during the Depression. He didn't work again until my mother started her own business ten years later and employed Ma and Da so they would have some income.

When we moved to the house in Waverley, Da would walk there from Vaucluse most days to have a cup of tea with my mother, and then walk back again. It was more than 20 miles each way, and it would take him all day. He would sometimes catch a bus for part of the way, and would often sit on the benches at the bus stops to rest. He had a habit of sleeping with his mouth and eyes open, and it was no surprise when one day Mum got a phone call from the local police to say Da had passed away at a bus stop. My mother was shocked when she went down to identify him, and found him sitting up drinking a cup of tea and eating a biscuit. This happened several times, and on one occasion when my dad took the call from a policeman he asked, "Are you sure? The old bugger has a habit of coming back." Dad was right. Da was just sleeping again.

I liked the way Da was interested in people and often stopped to talk to neighbors, admiring their gardens and asking after their families. Everyone had a soft spot for him. I think he spoke to other people more than he spoke to any of us. He had the ability to just be. He loved to stop and listen to the ocean crash against the rocks at the bluff. He enjoyed walks in Waverley Cemetery looking at the headstones of famous people. He would just take in the day. He never had a bad word to say about anyone. I certainly admired his tolerance and peace. He didn't seem to hold on to anything. He was OK with how things were, whether good or bad. He always knew it would work out. I think you learn a lot in 90 years. One thing I remember him saying was, "No one can ever hurt you unless you let them." That has always stuck with me.

He had a brass bell that looked like Queen Victoria, and would ring it when he was ready for his tea. I still have his brass bell on my shelf and I wouldn't let it go for anything.

#223 - YOUR GENERATION

<u>Which generation is yours?</u>
- The "Greatest Generation"
- Beat Generation
- Baby Boomers
- Generation X
- Millennials

<u>How does being a member of this generation define you?</u>
- What do you have in common with other members of your generation?
- How are you different from other members of your generation?

Your notes:_____

_____

_____

_____

#224 - GIFTS (1)

<u>What is the best gift you ever gave?</u>
- What is the gift you gave that fell absolutely flat?

<u>What is the best gift you ever received?</u>

<u>What gift were you given that you would willingly "re-gift" or donate to charity because it was absolutely wrong for you?</u>
- How did it make you feel to be given the "wrong" gift - especially if the gift was from someone you thought knew you well?

<u>What is the gift you wished for but never received?</u>
- The puppy or pony you wanted as a kid
- Your first car
- A special Valentine's Day gift
- An engagement ring

<u>As a child, what disappointing but practical gifts did you always get for holidays or your birthday?</u>
- Socks and underwear

- Tooth brush and tooth paste
- Stamps
- School supplies
- Tools
- Kitchen and housekeeping equipment
- Clothes
- Or?

Your notes:_____

_____

_____

_____

#225 - GIFTS (2)

<u>What do you think about when you shop for gifts?</u>
- Love
- Obligation
- Resentment
- Memories
- Happiness

<u>What gifts do you make rather than buy?</u>
- Baked goods
- Hand crafts
- Personal messages and poems
- Or?

Your notes:_____

_____

_____

_____

#226 - GIFTS (3)

"On the first day of Christmas, my true love gave to me a partridge in a pear tree."

- TRADITIONAL -

Describe a gift you received from your true love
- What were your feelings when you received this gift?

Describe a gift you gave to your true love
- What were your feelings when you gave this gift?

Your notes:_____

_____

_____

_____

#227 - DIVINE

The ancient Hindu expression "Namaste" means "I see the divine spark within you."

What is your divine spark?
What divine spark do you see in others?

Your notes:_____

_____

_____

_____

#228 - FAITH

<u>Describe your personal philosophy of faith</u>
- Do you believe in God?
- Has your concept of God changed as you've aged? How?
- If you do not believe in God, do you have a concept of a higher power?
- Do you believe you have a soul?

<u>Do you practice your faith within a traditional religion?</u>
- What religion?
- How does your religion help you develop faith?

<u>Do you practice religion in your home?</u>
- As a child
- As an adult
- Now

<u>If you do not practice an organized religion, how would you describe your faith?</u>
- Concept of a deity or deities
- Influence of nature
- Moral and ethical code

<u>Did you once have faith that you no longer have?</u>
- What caused you to lose your faith?

<u>Were you raised in a religious tradition that you stopped practicing, and then later returned to?</u>
- What caused you to fall away from your religious traditions?
- What caused you to return to your religious traditions later in life?

Your notes:_____

_____

_____

_____

#229 - QUESTIONS

<u>Do you have any questions to ask of someone in heaven?</u>
- What are your questions?
- Who would you ask?

Your notes:_____

_____

_____

_____

#230 - ANIMALS AND FAITH

<u>Do animals have a place in your concept of faith?</u>
- Do you believe animals have a soul?

<u>Will you meet well-loved pets on the "Rainbow Bridge"?</u>

Your notes:_____

_____

_____

_____

#231 - AFTERLIFE

<u>What are your beliefs about life after death?</u>
- Do you believe in Heaven?
- Hell?

<u>What do you hope or expect will happen after you die?</u>
- You will meet loved ones who predeceased you
- You will be able to communicate with the living

<u>Do you believe in reincarnation?</u>
- If you believe in reincarnation, what do you hope for in your next life?

Your notes:_____

_____

_____

_____

#232 - SCAR (2)

<u>Scars can be both emotional and physical. What is the story of one of your scars?</u>

Your notes:_____

_____

_____

_____

#233 - POETRY

"The vast majority of people find their only poetry in a good bellyful of food."

- Harry Kemp -

❈

Where do you find your poetry?

Your notes:_____

_____

_____

_____

#234 - SINS

The traditional seven deadly sins are wrath, greed, sloth, pride, lust, envy, and gluttony.

What are your personal deadly sins?

Your notes:_____

_____

_____

_____

#235 - SUMMER VACATION

Remember when you had "summer vacations", and after returning to school in the fall your first assignment would be to write about what you did over the summer? Here it is again!

<u>What did you do this summer?</u>
- Does what you did this summer remind you of how you spent summers when you were a child?

Your notes:_____

_____

_____

_____

#236 - FANTASY (1)

<u>Describe the fantasy you:</u>
- Royal or aristocrat
- President, political leader, or diplomat
- Chef
- Spy
- Astronaut
- Explorer or world traveler
- Inventor or scientist
- Athlete
- Best-selling author
- Actor or movie star
- Doctor or surgeon
- Teacher
- Parent
- Spouse
- Singer, musician, or artist

- Rich person
- "Free spirit"
- Or?

<u>What attracts you about the idea of being this person?</u>

- What would you do if you were this person?

<u>How are you like this person?</u>

Your notes:_____

_____

_____

_____

ELEVEN

HELPFUL HINT #26 - REMEMBER THANKFULNESS

Get yourself a small notebook. Write in your notebook every day at least five things for which you are thankful. These do not have to be huge things, and sometimes you may have to push yourself to find thankfulness. When this happens, try saying thanks for small things, such as "Today I am thankful I drove safely," or "Today I am thankful that I have a pet." Just say thank you.

This will help you in a few ways. First, it will get you in the habit of writing every day. If you do no other writing, spending a few minutes to record your thanks will serve to get you writing. Secondly, recording your thanks may help you remember things you want to include in your autobiography. If you write "Today I am thankful I drove safely," it may lead to memories of learning to drive, your first car, road trips, car accidents and tickets, teaching your children to drive, and other car related memories. Use your notebook to record your thanks, but also be open to its use as a tool to help you remember.

And finally, expressing gratitude will help your attitude. It will help lighten your thoughts and present a more positive you to the world. And there is certainly nothing wrong with that!

#237 - GRATITUDE

<u>What are you the most grateful for in your life?</u>
<u>What are you the most grateful for right now?</u>

Your notes:_____

_____

_____

_____

#238 - THANKFULNESS (1)

<u>Who are the people in your life to whom you are grateful?</u>
- Family and friends who are a daily presence in your life
- People you wish you had thanked but didn't
- People you have thanked but want to thank again
- People who did something special for you
- People who continue to do special things for you
- People who have been a long-term source of support and comfort

<u>Who are the people you thanked but want to thank again?</u>
- Why are you still thankful?

<u>Who are the people you wish you had thanked but didn't?</u>
- What did these people do?

Your notes:_____

_____

_____

_____

"Life is Full of the Unexpected"
by Joy Karsevar

I never thought when I moved to Upland that I would be signing up for an autobiography class. Not once did I wake up and declare to myself, "I just have to tell my life story!" I have a senior friend who wrote her autobiography, and even had it published and I thought that was great, but that was her and not me! I was happy just living life.

As I sit here today, surrounded by a group of wonderful writers and women who are human, and yet so talented and brave, I cannot help but feel so grateful that I came to Upland and took the Art of Autobiography class. This class has enabled me to see myself and my life in a better light and given me the courage and skill to write my life story. I was able to deal with parts of my life story I may not have wanted to, but I am sure glad I did. My story, as with everyone's story, has to be remembered, written, revisited, relived in my mind and heart and definitely enjoyed and passed down to loved ones and in my case, my husband Alan and children Alice and Mason, as well as my relatives, friends, and future generations of my family.

Aside from writing my story, I learned so much from my colleagues in class. Their own life stories helped me remember stories in my own life that I may have neglected or even forgotten. The stories also made me see how our lives are all interconnected. In the process a wonderful thing happened. I made new friends and got to have real down-to-earth connections with my new found friends. I got to cry with them and also laugh with them. I felt so wonderfully alive in this class.

I want to thank each one of you for your friendship, openness, and trust. I will always treasure you and our times together. I will miss you so much and I will miss our special group. But who knows, since I am kinda a gypsy and a pirate lady at heart, you may just see me back in Upland or in your future travels; hopefully in the Caribbean with a rum drink in hand. Til then ... I am just an email away.

#239 - THANKFULNESS (2)

<u>Sometimes you may find thankfulness in disaster or disappointment</u>
- It could have been so much worse
- I lived through it
- I had the support and love of family and friends
- We all lived through it
- No one was hurt too badly
- We will survive
- We will rebuild

<u>Where did you find thankfulness in a dark hour?</u>

Your notes:_____

_____

_____

_____

#240 - GADGET

<u>Write about a gadget or invention that makes your life easier</u>
- Credit cards
- Computers and the internet
- Post-it notes
- Staples and paper clips
- Appliances: refrigerator, stove, washer and dryer, microwave, dishwasher
- Cars
- Airplanes
- Electricity and light blubs
- Telephones, smart phones, tablets, I-pads
- Indoor plumbing
- Modern medical equipment
- Air conditioning
- Television

<u>How old were you when you first used this invention?</u>
- How did this invention change your life?

Your notes:_____

_____

_____

_____

HELPFUL HINT #27 - ENGAGEMENT

Take a look at some of the books you love. What kept you reading beyond the first chapter? What engaged you so that you wanted to know more about the characters, whether real or fictional?

I recently read two memoirs in which both authors went to Maine on a voyage of self-discovery. In the first memoir, the author did a lot of, "Ooh - look at the birds, ooh - look at the beavers, ooh - look at the logs." His disengagement from his own life made the story dull and lackluster. The other book, while similar, was interesting and engaging because the author wove the facts *of* her life into thoughts *about* her life, giving me, the reader, a real sense of who she was.

No one lives their life in one note. You go to many different places and do many different things. In writing your memoirs, it is important to bring in the *entire* experience of being you. Even if you spent a summer alone in Maine discovering yourself, other things would intrude. You can't spend the entire time staring at your belly button. Eventually some thought has to be given to what's for dinner.

You have written a successful memoir when your reader says, "I wish I knew that person better."

#241 - AND THE WINNER IS

<u>If you could give yourself an award or prize what would it be?</u>
- Nobel prize
- Academy award
- Grammy or CMA
- Edgar, Agatha, Anthony, or Hugo
- Pulitzer
- Emmy
- Scouting badge
- Olympic medal
- Heisman trophy
- Tony or Obie
- Mother or Father of the year
- Employee of the month
- Or?

<u>What did you do to win this award?</u>
<u>Write your acceptance speech</u>

Your notes:_____

_____

_____

_____

#242 - ADVICE

<u>What is the best piece of advice you've been given?</u>
<u>What is the best piece of advice you gave to someone else?</u>

Your notes:_____

_____

_____

_____

#243 - PAST

Think about who you were at age 25, and give that person some advice
If the person you were at 25 had listened to and followed that advice, what difference would it have made?
- To your life?
- To your career?
- To your relationships?
- To your finances?
- To where you now live?

Your notes:_____

_____

_____

_____

#244 - BELIEVE IT OR NOT

"You may not believe it, but this really happened to me"
- Describe what happened
What makes it so unbelievable?

Your notes:_____

_____

_____

_____

#245 - UNEXPECTED PLEASURES

<u>Is there something you were never going to do, but when you tried it, found you enjoyed it or were glad you did it?</u>
- Never going to try a particular food
- Never going to have a pedicure or color your hair
- Never going to see the movies of that actor
- You're a dog person and will never have a cat
- Never take that type of vacation
- Never listen to that type of music
- Never read a book by that author
- Never go out with that person
- Never take that kind of job
- Never engage in that sport
- Never have cosmetic surgery
- Or?

<u>What was it about this activity that you thought you would dislike?</u>
<u>What convinced you to finally try it?</u>
- Describe the experience of trying it for the first time
- What did you enjoy about it?

<u>Now that you know you like doing this thing, will you do it again?</u>

Your notes:_____

_____

_____

_____

"Shrimp? I would never get close, touch or eat that thing!"
by Luna

A long time ago, my husband and I decided to take a road trip from Lima, Peru, to Buenos Aires, Argentina in a VW, camping and surfing along the Pacific Coast. We did not have children and we were taking the three months of summer for the trip. The second day of the trip, I started to feel funny, very sleepy and nauseated and tired. My husband said it was too much driving and the heat, and we would take it easier. We spent two days in our next stop walking around town and eating good meals.

The next day we continued toward the Peru-Chile border. We started noticing people along the road, offering baskets containing something. When we slowed to see what it was they were selling, their baskets were empty. We continued driving, and when we got closer to the town of Camana, the baskets showed up again. We stopped and asked what it was they were selling and they said it was fresh water shrimp. My husband asked, "Where is the shrimp? I want to see it." I said, "Shrimp?? I am scared of shrimp! They are alive, I hate shrimp and I don't want to see them or take any in the car with me!"

We continued driving despite my husband's arguments to convince me it was safe and the shrimp would not be walking all over me. We decided to find a hotel in town to spend the night because we needed a good rest. As soon as we got to the hotel room, I said, "I want shrimp." My husband said, "It will have to be tomorrow. I am tired and it is a 45 minute drive back to find them, even if they stay this late. And anyway, the hotel kitchen is closed." He went to sleep. I could not sleep. I had never been close to a shrimp, let alone eat one, but I craved those shrimp like there was no tomorrow.

I jumped in the car and drove back, found them, bought a two pound basket of shrimp and put it in the car with me! I then drove back to the hotel. It was 11:30 p.m. I managed to get the camping stove upstairs, along with the propane tank, a pot, utensils, and a plate. I cleaned the shrimp and started boiling them. I didn't know how to make a dish with them, and did not have any spices or even salt. Besides, I just hated those things.

When I started to smell the aroma, I could not wait, and started eating the shrimp, and found them so delicious! I ate the whole two pound basket! Then I went to sleep like an angel.

The next morning, when I told my husband about the shrimp, he said, "You must be pregnant. It can't be that you now crave shrimp out of the blue." Over breakfast we remembered how tired, sleepy and nauseated I had been. I went to see a doctor when we arrived in Antofagasta, Chile. I <u>was</u> pregnant!

#246 - ANOTHER LIFE

<u>What other person's life would you like to lead?</u>
- Famous person
- Family member
- Friend

<u>Why would you like to lead this person's life?</u>
- How is your real life like this person's life?
- How is your real life different from this person's life?

Your notes:_____

_____

_____

_____

#247 - FICTIONAL

<u>What fictional or cartoon character would you like to be?</u>
- What about this character attracts you?

<u>How are you like this character in your real life?</u>

Your notes:_____

_____

_____

_____

#248 - ON-LINE

<u>Write your dating profile for Match.com</u>
- Seeking a long-term relationship or just want to have some fun
- Your positive personality traits
- Your hobbies and interests
- A physical description of yourself
- What you absolutely will not accept in a partner

<u>What attracts you to a person enough to want to pursue a relationship?</u>
- Sense of humor
- Brains
- Certain physical characteristics
- Shared interests
- Common religious or political beliefs
- "Opposites attract"

Even if you are not interested in posting an on-line dating profile, this exercise helps you express in just a few words how you view yourself, your interests, and your values.

Your notes:_____

_____

_____

_____

#249 - ACCIDENTAL

<u>Describe an accidental masterpiece</u>

Your notes:_____

_____

_____

_____

TWELVE

HELPFUL HINT #28 - LISTEN TO OTHERS

If you are in a writing group, autobiography class, or just chatting with friends, be sure to listen when others share their stories. Pay attention to what is said, rather than rehearsing in your head what *you* will say and how *you* will respond. Not only are other peoples' stories interesting and well worth hearing, their stories may also remind you of stories from your own life.

Listening is not only polite - it also helps you remember.

#250 - LISTEN

<u>Are you heard?</u>
- When do you feel voiceless?
- Who listens to you?
- Who doesn't listen to you?

Your notes:_____

_____

_____

_____

#251 - MOTHER'S DAY / FATHER'S DAY

<u>What is the favorite Mother's Day or Father's Day gift:</u>
- You ever received?
- You ever gave?

<u>What Mother's Day or Father's Day gift do you **wish** you had received?</u>

<u>Is there a sentiment you **wish** you had expressed on Mother's Day or Father's Day?</u>
- What do you want to say?
- To whom are you saying it?
- What prevented you from expressing your sentiments the first time?

Your notes:_____

_____

_____

_____

✠

"My Mother"
by Dorothy Timm Sasine

I've looked the field all over, on
this bright Mother's day -

To find a card that means just
what I'd like to say -
The thoughts are sentimental, and
every word is true -
But in my estimation, just not good
enough for you.

I think back to the yesterdays, and
the many things you've done -
The many times I worried you, and
kept you on the run -
I didn't think about it then, but I
certainly do now -
Your love was always with me,
you understood somehow.

Today you haven't changed, you're still
so good and fine -
Tomorrow you'll be just the same,
growing dearer with time -
My love is with you always, not just
one day a year -

To me each day is your own day,
God Bless You Mother Dear.

To Martha Aschenbach Timm Kennedy
Mother's Day, 1944

#252 - SHORTFALL

<u>One time when I was desperate for cash, I —</u>
- Begged
- Sold my blood
- Pawned my possessions
- Turned a trick
- Borrowed from the wrong person

<u>What happened to make you so short of cash?</u>
<u>How did you get back on your feet?</u>

Your notes:_____

_____

_____

_____

#253 - UNIFORM

<u>Describe a time when you wore a uniform</u>
- School
- Girl Scouts or Boy Scouts
- Military service
- For a job

Your notes:_____

_____

_____

_____

#254 - FAILURE

<u>Describe a time you failed</u>
- Did you try again?
- If you did try again, did you succeed?

<u>If you did not try again, why not?</u>

Remember success is not only achieving what you set out to do, it is also having the courage to re-examine your desires and expectations, and set new goals for yourself. Sometimes failure is a way of telling your heart to look elsewhere.

Your notes:_____

_____

_____

_____

#255 - SOMETHING SAID

<u>Has someone said one thing to you that changed your life?</u>
- What was said?
- Who said it?

<u>Was it a good piece of advice?</u>
<u>How did it change your life?</u>
- Was the result of this change positive or negative?

Your notes:_____

_____

_____

_____

#256 - UNWELCOME SURPRISE

<u>I didn't think it would happen, but it did</u>
- Foreclosure
- Financial failure
- Job loss
- Unexpected or sudden loss of a spouse or child
- Troubled or troublesome children
- Catastrophic illness or injury to yourself or another
- Or?

<u>I expected this to happen, but it never did</u>
- Job success
- Marriage and children
- Or?

<u>This is how I dealt with it</u>

Your notes:_____

_____

_____

_____

✶

HELPFUL HINT #29 - BE OPEN

It's hard to be objective about your own writing. For a long time I thought <u>everything</u> I wrote was wonderful. Then I re-read my writings and thought everything I wrote was garbage. Now my opinion of my own writing is more balanced. Some of it is good, some is bad, some is OK, and a lot of it needs more work.

Don't get overly attached to the way you tell your story or to your own writing style. You want your writing to reflect your true voice, but if you become too attached, you will be deaf to good advice offered by others that may improve your story.

#257 - INTELLIGENCE

<u>What kind of intelligence do you have?</u>
- Book learning
- Emotional intelligence
- Intuitive intelligence
- Empathy or sympathy
- Creative intelligence
- "Street smarts"
- Good sense

<u>What kind of intelligence do you lack?</u>

Your notes:_____

_____

_____

_____

#258 - KEY

<u>Your key to happiness is ...</u>

Your notes:_____

_____

_____

_____

#259 - WISHING (1)

<u>What do you wish you could do?</u>
- Play an instrument or sing
- Write a bestseller
- Win an Oscar, Nobel Prize, or Olympic medal
- Climb Mount Everest
- Bike across the country
- Hike the Appalachian Trail
- Play in a championship athletic contest
- Star in a movie or Broadway show
- Meet a famous person
- Be a famous person
- Give a speech
- Or?

<u>What could you do to fulfill your wish?</u>

Your notes:_____

_____

_____

_____

#260 - WISHING (2)

<u>What do you wish was true?</u>

Your notes:_____

_____

_____

_____

#261 - FAME

How are you famous?
- Are you well know within your own area of expertise?

For what would you like to become famous?

Your notes:_____

_____

_____

_____

#262 - WALKING

Go take a walk, then write about your thoughts

Your notes:_____

_____

_____

_____

#263 - PACKING (1)

If you had five minutes to pack a suitcase and leave your home, what would you take?

Your notes:_____
_____
_____
_____

#264 - PACKING (2)

<u>What things do you always pack to take on a trip?</u>

Your notes:_____
_____
_____
_____

#265 - SUPERNATURAL

<u>Have you ever seen a ghost?</u>
- Have you ever been haunted by a ghost?

<u>Have you ever had a paranormal experience?</u>

Your notes:_____
_____
_____
_____

#266 - HEROISM

Living your life with integrity and honesty is heroic. Doing the best you can do every day is heroic.

How are you heroic?

Your notes:_____

_____

_____

_____

⚬⚬

"True Heroes"
by Ann Hamer

An email came to me a few months ago from my English university. "Nominate our most successful alumnus," it invited. Graduates of this university are presidents and prime ministers, senators and investors and writers and scientists and educators and entrepreneurs. A former friend from my university days served in President Obama's cabinet. Is that success? I usually think so.

A few days after I received this email, I had to go to the lab for a blood test. It's routine for me now, so unless the technician is digging away poking and prodding at my shy and rolling veins, I am not apprehensive. Instead, I wait and I watch. I watch the blue collar workers in flannels and huaraches waiting for their pre-employment drug screens, and I watch the kids there for their pre-school blood harvest. I watch the bitty babies, scared and hurting, not understanding the process or their pain, their fear exacerbated by the tsking and clucking of well meaning adults.

On this particular day, two Filipino men came in, each with a very obviously mentally disabled young man for whom he was caring. The disabled understood the process no better than the babies, but were bigger, stronger, and better able to flee. They did not understand they were to pee in a cup, not on the floor, not on the toilet rim, and not down their leg. They didn't understand the tiny sting was as fleeting as the disposable butterfly needle the tech used. The purple band tightens around the upper arm, thump thump *to raise the vein, the kiss of the needle, the blood in the vial, and then it's done. Hold the cotton tight, the tech wraps some tape around your arm, and then you go home.*

But not for the disabled men. After the struggle to pee in the cup, the caretakers led their charges to the chairs where their blood would be taken. Fumble resisting the band. Fumble resisting the needle. Fumble with the cotton ball. Fumble with the discomfort.

And through it all, these two caretakers were angels. Endless smiles. Gently steering their disabled charges beyond their discomfort and their fear and their confusion. Smiling at me, smiling at the techs and the nurses and the receptionists and the other people waiting to be tested. Smiling and encouraging us all.

I thought about success. At my fancy pants English university these two men would have been considered failures. Schlepping around the disabled? You're not a surgeon or a scholar or a Nobel laureate? What a failure.

They're just kind
And gentle
And patient
And understanding
And sweet
Unremittingly sweet
And absolutely excellent and good and committed to what they do.

And <u>that</u> is success.

THIRTEEN

HELPFUL HINT #30 - BE PERSISTENT

Writing is all about persistence. Keep at it and be open to feedback from others. Remember, even J.K. Rowling was told not to quit her day job, and submitted *Harry Potter and the Sorcerer's Stone* to twelve publishers before it was finally accepted.

#267 - YOUR HERO

<u>Describe the traits and characteristics of a super-hero you create</u>
- What is the name of your super-hero?

<u>What is the form of your super-hero?</u>
- Human
- Animal or insect
- Mechanical or robotic
- Extra-terrestrial
- Or?

<u>What characteristics do you share with your super-hero?</u>

Your notes:_____

_____

_____

_____

#268 - ACCEPT YOURSELF

<u>When did you stop comparing yourself to other people?</u>
- What happened to make you accept yourself as you are?

Your notes:_____

_____

_____

_____

#269 - DINNER PARTY

<u>Describe your ideal dinner party</u>
- A perfect dinner party you hosted
- A perfect dinner party you attended
- The fantasy dinner party you would host

<u>Who was there?</u>
- What food was served?
- When and where was it held?
- What topics were discussed?

<u>What made it so perfect?</u>

Your notes:_____

_____

_____

_____

#270 - CRUELTY

<u>Was there something said to you or something you said to someone else that you find difficult to forget or forgive?</u>
- A time when you said or did something cruel, even if it was unintentional
- A time when someone said or did something cruel to you which still hurts and you still remember

Your notes:_____

_____

_____

_____

HELPFUL HINT #31 - YOU MAY NOT BE AS FUNNY AS YOU THINK

Have you ever said something you thought was funny, only to have it fall flat or hurt another person? You want to be aware of the *tone* of your writing. You do not want something you think is funny or clever to come across as snide, cruel, or mean spirited.

Reading your material out loud will help you hear the tone of your writing.

#271 - CHANGING WORLD OF HEALTH

<u>What diseases and illnesses have been conquered or at least become more manageable since you were a child?</u>
- Polio
- Infections
- Cancer
- Dangers associated with childbirth
- Flu

<u>Did you have a friend or relative who died or was disabled, who probably would have survived today?</u>

<u>How will your senior years be different from those of your parents or grandparents?</u>
- Expectation of an active and healthy retirement
- Expectation of a longer life than your parents or grandparents

Your notes:_____

_____

_____

_____

#272 - LIFE LESSON

<u>What life lesson or profound truth did you learn from a serious or life threatening illness or injury?</u>
- Strength
- Perseverance
- How much you are loved and supported by others
- Ability to deal with profound loss
- Strength of character
- Assertiveness
- Or?

Your notes:_____

_____

_____

_____

#273 - LESSONS (1)

<u>What lessons did you learn from difficult times?</u>
- From someone's death
- From losing a job
- From a divorce or break-up
- Or?

Your notes:_____

_____

_____

_____

#274 - LESSONS (2)

<u>What lessons did you learn from happy times?</u>

Your notes:_____

_____

_____

_____

#275 - CHARM

<u>The third time's a charm</u>

Your notes:_____

_____

_____

_____

❈

HELPFUL HINT #32 - RESIST COMPARISONS

Resist the temptation to compare yourself to others. It is self-defeating and can lead to inertia and procrastination. There will always be better writers than you, just as you are a better writer than some others.

Your goal is to tell your story. If you give in to a temptation to make comparisons, you may end up discouraged, stop writing, and not tell your story at all.

❈

#276 - UNIQUE

<u>What makes your family unique?</u>
<u>What makes you unique?</u>

Your notes:_____

_____

_____

_____

#277 - DOING RIGHT

<u>Write about a time when you did the right thing</u>

Your notes:_____

_____

_____

_____

#278 - RELIEF

<u>"It was such a relief when I no longer had to . . . "</u>
- Did you feel a sense of freedom or release when you no longer had to do this thing?
- Did you feel any sense of loss or sadness in addition to your relief?

Your notes:_____

_____

_____

_____

#279 - CIRCUMSTANCES

<u>How have your circumstances changed as you've aged?</u>
- Empty nester
- Death of a spouse
- Income changes
- Caregiver for spouse, parent, or sibling
- Retiree vs. member of the workforce
- Grandparent vs. parent
- And?

<u>How have these changes affected you?</u>
- Do you feel less important or less valuable due to these changes?

Your notes:_____

_____

_____

_____

"Journal of My New Life"
by M.B.

I wanted to do and accomplish so many things when I was young and I did most. But still, as soon as I retired from the job I had been doing all my life, I took the autobiography class and then registered for a sign language class at Cirrus College.

I went to Cirrus with a friend who took the sign language class to practice, and I took it because I've always wanted to learn one more language. In the class I had an excellent instructor who gave me the confidence to express myself with my hands. She told me that my personality comes on very strong when I'm signing. As an experienced sign language teacher she understands, but for a novice or my cohorts in class it looks as if I'm signing letters twice. It was fun and challenging at the same time. I learned something new and it was very hard, but in the end I was able to say a small history with my hands.

#280 - TATTOO

<u>Do you have a tattoo?</u>
- What is it?
- Where is it?

<u>How old were you when you got your first tattoo?</u>
- Do you have more than one tattoo?

Why did you get a tattoo?
* Do you have any regrets over getting a tattoo?

If you were to get a tattoo today, where and what would it be?

Your notes:_____

_____

_____

_____

#281 - BLINDSIDED

Write about a time when you didn't see it coming

Your notes:_____

_____

_____

_____

HELPFUL HINT #33 - MAKING LISTS

Making lists may help jog your memory. Your lists can bring to mind people and things you have not thought about for many years.

Here are some suggestions for lists to work on
* Books read
* Movies seen
* Places visited
* Concerts, plays, or sporting events attended

- Classes taken
- Toys and games played
- Pets and animals you've known

#282 - MONEY

<u>Describe your attitude toward money</u>
- You can never have enough, and some people might call you "money hungry"
- Having enough money for financial security is all you really need; sometimes more than enough is just "too much"
- You've never had enough money, and that has made life difficult

<u>Have any relationships been ruined because of your attitude toward money?</u>

Your notes:_____

_____

_____

_____

#283 - JOY

<u>What gives you your greatest joy?</u>
- What makes you smile?

Your notes:_____

_____

_____

_____

#284 - MUSIC

"Sometimes it's the artist's task to find out how much music you can make with what you have left."

- Itzhak Perlman -

How much music do you have left?
- What is the sound of your music?
- How can you express your music?

Will you express your music with an instrument, your voice, or is it metaphorical music you hold in your heart?

Your notes:_____

_____

_____

_____

#285 - REVENGE

Have you ever been so angry you wanted to hurt someone?
- Who?
- Why?

What happened to make you want to take revenge?

Did you ever plot revenge?
- Did you carry out your plot?

Your notes:_____

_____

_____

_____

❧

"Placing a Curse"
by Barbara Cauthorn

Thoughts of homicide can occur even to peaceable, animal loving vegetarians. I have no experience with homicide, although I expect it's rather messy. I hate a mess, so maybe it's not a feasible course of action. I'm going to put a curse on him instead. By "him" I'm referring to my cousin. Co-beneficiary of his mother's estate. The estate I am the executor of. He is a person with no conscience.

An internet search reveals that, "Putting a curse on someone might cause you to enter a dark world of evil." No. Absolutely not. Another search suggests, "Send them love and forgiveness." No, that's not going to work either.

"A Simple Voodoo Hex Using Common Household Items." Ah! Just right. The goal is to foil someone's harmful plans, not to cause actual harm. Suggested targets are bullies, pain-in-the-neck neighbors, and intractable bigots.

I gathered cayenne pepper, tap water, candles, and a sturdy plastic Baggie. Then I wrote his name on a slip of paper. I waited for darkness and lit the candles. The cayenne pepper and a good slosh of water went into the Baggie, followed by the slip of paper. Securely seal the Baggie. We're ready to go.

Vigorously shake the Baggie like you're making cocktails. Stomp your feet forcefully.

"Open the Gate, spirits!" "Open the Gate!" "Jerry, I bind and confound your evil plans!!"

Continue stomping and shaking and yelling. Repeat until you feel that it's working. Thank the spirits and request them to close the Gate.

I blew out the candles, put the Baggie in the freezer (to be carefully disposed of later) and went to bed. It was my first good night's sleep in months.

A few days later, I began to itch. I'd recently returned from a road trip, and my first thought was, "Oh my god, bedbugs!" from highway motels. I stripped the bed, washed everything in hot water and bleach, vacuumed, inspected, washed and scrubbed some more. My goodness, my house was clean! Days went by. I still itched. I visited the walk-in clinic at the local Wal-mart.

"Dermatitis," he said. "My wife gets it, too. Every winter."

"I was afraid it was bedbugs," I said.

"Oh no," he said cheerfully, and wrote a prescription.

I'd never had dermatitis before. It's summer now and the itch has not gone away. If anything, it's gotten worse. I don't know what happened to my cousin. It's not like he confides in me.

#286 - FREE DAY

<u>What would you do on a day with no obligations, no appointments, and nothing you absolutely had to do?</u>

Your notes:_____

_____

_____

_____

#287 - INSIDER

Describe a time when you felt like an insider or a member of the "in" crowd

Your notes:_____

_____

_____

_____

#288 - OUTSIDER

Describe a time when you felt like an outsider

Your notes:_____

_____

_____

_____

#289 - CANDLE

In her poem, "First Fig", Edna St. Vincent Millay wrote, "My candle burns at both ends; it will not last the night."

Does your candle burn at both ends or just one end?
- Will your candle last the night?
- Do you have no candle at all?
- My light's blown out!

Your notes:_____

_____

_____

_____

#290 - ANSWERS

Why
- I did (or did not) get that job
- I did (or did not) get that part
- I did (or did not) get chosen for the team
- That person did (or did not) love me
- They forgot I was there

Your notes:_____

_____

_____

_____

#291 - OUT OF CONTROL

What are your addictions?
- Food
- Alcohol
- Drugs

- Shopping
- Sex
- Exercise
- Or?

<u>Do you have any bad habits you can't seem to break?</u>
- Procrastination
- Lazing in bed all day
- Or?

<u>How have your addictions and bad habits impacted your life?</u>
- Money issues
- Job loss
- Health issues
- Relationship loss
- Embarrassment
- Caused harm to yourself or others
- And?

Your notes:_____

_____

_____

_____

Fourteen

As you read the memoirs and autobiographies of others, notice the difference between a story that engages you and one that leaves you flat. I think the difference is enthusiasm. You can't stand apart from your life when you're telling your story. If you tell your story with energy and enthusiasm, it will come alive for your readers.

Be interested in what you write. If you don't care about your story, don't expect others to care. If you don't find yourself interesting, your readers won't find you interesting either.

#292 - HOORAY FOR ME

<u>What do you like about yourself?</u>

Your notes:_____

_____

_____

_____

#293 - GOOD DEED

<u>Write about a time you performed a good deed</u>
- What did you do?
- Who benefitted?

Your notes:_____

_____

_____

_____

#294 - HUMAN BEAUTY

<u>Who is the most beautiful or handsome person you ever met?</u>
- Does this person have inner beauty, outer beauty, or both?

<u>How do you feel about yourself when you are around this person?</u>
- Confident - we're all beautiful in some way
- Insecure
- I feel no differently about myself than I usually feel

Your notes:_____

_____

_____

_____

#295 - GUARDIAN

<u>Describe your Guardian Angel</u>
- Female, male, or asexual being
- Human or non-human form
- Wings?

<u>How do you experience the presence of this angel in your life?</u>
- Has your guardian angel preformed miracles in your life?

<u>Do you pray to your guardian angel?</u>

Your notes:_____

_____

_____

_____

#296 - MUSICAL

<u>What instrument do you play?</u>
- How long have you been playing this instrument?
- Why did you choose to study this instrument?

<u>Did you sing in a school, church, or community choir?</u>

<u>Have you ever been a solo artist?</u>
- Describe your solo performance(s)

<u>Do you still play the instrument or sing?</u>
- If not, why?

Your notes:_____

_____

_____

_____

#297 - NEXT

<u>What's next?</u>

Your notes:_____

_____

_____

_____

#298 - GOALS

<u>Describe a goal you set for yourself and achieved</u>
<u>Do you have goals you have not achieved?</u>
- Are you continuing to try to achieve these goals?

Your notes:_____

_____

_____

_____

❧

HELPFUL HINT #35 - WATCH YOUR WORD CHOICE

You want to write with your authentic voice, but confrontational, abusive, or offensive language, or using words solely for their shock value may be inappropriate, and make your readers dislike you. In a conversation, if you said, "Fuck you, John," then using that language gives your readers a true sense of the intensity of your emotions because it is what you actually said. Choose words for their effectiveness so you communicate precisely what you mean to say. Don't use words in a way that is so offensive it makes your readers dislike you and your memoir.

Of course, you need to be wary of losing your impact through over-sanitation. "A bear shit in the woods," is much more effective than, "The ursine creature defecated in the undergrowth."

Remember though, a little bear poop goes a long way.

❧

#299 - COMPLIMENTS

<u>What is the best compliment you ever received?</u>
<u>What is the best compliment you ever gave?</u>

Your notes:_____
_____
_____
_____

#300 - UNLOVED (1)

<u>When did you realize that you weren't the love of his or her life?</u>
• Do you still have feelings for this person?

Your notes:_____
_____
_____
_____

#301 - UNLOVED (2)

<u>Were you ever loved by someone you did not love?</u>
• How did you tell this person you did not love him or her?

<u>Were you able to be friends with this person?</u>

Your notes:_____

_____

_____

_____

#302 - NAME CALLING

<u>Were you ever called names?</u>
- Sissy
- Bully
- Crybaby
- Tomboy
- Fatty
- Nerd
- Loser
- Stupid
- Ugly
- Or?

<u>How did it make you feel to be called names?</u>
- Who called you names?

<u>Did you ever confront the person who called you names?</u>
- What happened when you did?

<u>Did you ever call other people names?</u>
- Who did you call names?
- Why?
- How do you feel about that now?

Your notes:_____

_____

_____

_____

#303 - JUDGMENT

"I judge people on two things - do they tip and do they love dogs."

- ROBERT WUHL -

<u>On what do you judge people?</u>

Your notes:_____

_____

_____

_____

#304 - DIFFERENT

<u>In what ways are you different from other people?</u>
- Do you embrace your difference or would you rather be more like everyone else?

Your notes:_____

_____

_____

_____

#305 - FAMOUS PEOPLE

<u>Describe your encounters with famous people</u>

Your notes:_____

_____

_____

_____

HELPFUL HINT #36 - WRITE OUT NEGATIVITY

Memoir writing is sometimes a painful process. If you're a glass half empty sort of person, your tone may come across as angry, bitter, or depressing. You don't want your written legacy to be one of negativity.

Some of the exercises in this book may help you to write out your hurt. Write out your pain and feelings of anger, and then throw it away or file it, and start over again.

#306 - GUILTY

<u>About what do you feel guilty?</u>

Your notes:_____

_____

_____

_____

#307 - COMMUNICATIONS

<u>Describe the most exciting telephone call, letter, or e-mail you received</u>
- Job offer
- College acceptance
- Love letter
- Renewed contact from a long-lost relative or friend
- Unexpected money
- Announcement of an engagement
- Announcement of a pregnancy or birth
- Something you won
- Or?

Your notes:_____

_____

_____

_____

#308 - BEST PARTY

<u>Describe the best party you ever attended</u>
- What made it the best?
- Who was there?

- What was the reason for the party?
- Were you the host or a guest?

Your notes:_____

_____

_____

_____

❧

"The Pirate Ship"
by Joy Karsevar

Imagine a pirate ship ... that is where we were married. My husband to be, Alan Raymond Karsevar, built the pirate ship called "Brigantine Sultana" during his spare time with a group of volunteers in Richmond, California.

Alan and I would exchange our vows on Saturday August 11, 1984 aboard the Brigantine Sultana. Our ceremony was to be under sail from Alameda to San Francisco and back. The ship could only accommodate fifty people, so we limited the invitations for the wedding ceremony to that number. We invited 200 people to the reception which was to follow at the Encinal Yacht Club. Since the Sultana was an authentic replica of an 18th century vessel, we decided to dress up in that century's outfits and pirate attire. Alan and I had our wedding outfits tailor-made, and rented the entourage's outfits from a Berkeley costumer.

Alan's parents, Leonard and Evelyn Karsevar, came from southern California, while my parents, Ricardo and Ofelia Tomacruz flew in from the Philippines. We, together with our parents, were very excited as well as quite nervous and anxious. My mother asked to see my wedding gown and shocked, exclaimed upon seeing it, "This is not a wedding gown, this is a costume!" Nerves were all over the place before the wedding. There were a thousand and one details to attend to. What was most pressing was having to bring the Sultana to Alameda under motor (not sail) from Brisbane, where her home port was, two days before the wedding. Transporting the Sultana was a feat on its own. It is amazing we still had the energy to go on with the wedding.

By the grace of God, everything turned out beautifully. I walked down the dock beaming, with my favorite flower bouquet (gardenias), holding on to my Dad (honestly I think he could not believe he was giving his daughter away on a pirate ship.) Alan looked like a real 18th century captain, and was so excited to see me! All our relatives and close friends were so happy to celebrate the momentous occasion with us. The reverend who officiated could not believe his eyes when he saw the ship, and he enjoyed the ceremony and talked so much during the wedding message that we almost ran out of water to sail on.

We had more than fifty guests for the wedding ceremony, but luckily two other boats joined in with the rest of our guests. At the reception we had 200 guests. Food and drink flowed all day long. Everyone had a blast and no one wanted to go home. The celebration lasted from 9 a.m. to 4 p.m. and at the end everyone wanted to still hang around the ship. The grand finale was a gift from a couple of crew members who dressed in tuxedoes and went up to the crow's nest and jumped into the water.

What an unforgettable wedding! What a great start to our life together! People talked about our wedding for years!

#309 - PARTY

Write about a party you weren't invited to

Your notes:_____

_____

_____

_____

#310 - ANGER

What stresses or angers you?
* Is what stresses or angers you now different from when you were younger?

How do you now deal with your stress and anger?

Your notes:_____

_____

_____

_____

#311 - SPIRITUAL

Describe a profound and meaningful spiritual experience

Your notes:_____

_____

_____

_____

#312 - MIRACLE

Have you ever experienced a miracle?

To what do you attribute this miracle?
* God or other deity
* Guardian angel
* Luck
* Being in the right place at the right time
* There is no explanation

Your notes:_____

_____

_____

_____

#313 - ELECTED

<u>Describe a time when you won an election</u>
- Who was your competition?
- What was your campaign strategy?

<u>What were your honors and achievements while in office?</u>

Your notes:_____

_____

_____

_____

#314 - ALSO RAN

<u>Describe a time when you didn't win, came in last, or were an "also ran"</u>
- Did you try a second time, or was once enough?
- If you tried a second time, what happened?

Your notes:_____

_____

_____

_____

Fifteen

HELPFUL HINT #37 - MEMOIR VS. AUTOBIOGRAPHY

Mom and I call our class, "The Art of Autobiography", but in reality we teach a class in memoir writing. Memoir and autobiography are not the same thing. Autobiography is like Jack Webb in *Dragnet* - "Just the facts, Ma'am." Memoir records the stories of your life. It tells of the events that made you who you are, and helps others get to know you better.

When memoirists write stories about love, grandparents, growing up, a favorite outfit or party, pets, and career, not only do we get a sense of who they are as people, we also get a sense of their communities, their interests, and the people who surrounded them and formed the fabric of their lives. Recording when and where you were born, went to school, married, worked, resided, and traveled tells your readers just the facts. But it is the individual stories of your life that engage your readers and tell them who you truly are.

#315 - DEAR DIARY

<u>Write a diary entry or letter to yourself dated ten years from now</u>
- What will your life be like in ten years?

<u>Where will you be living?</u>

- Where you live now
- Moved to a larger home
- Moved to a more suburban or rural home
- Downsized and moved to a smaller home
- In a senior community
- Moved in with a child or friend

What will you be doing?

- Working
- Retired
- Volunteer work
- Traveling
- Spending more time with family and friends
- Learning a new sport or skill
- Writing a book
- Or?

How will you look?

- Describe the state of your health and well-being

Sum up your previous ten years of living in your diary entry or letter

- Things you hope you will have done
- Places you hope you will have visited
- Relationships you hope you will have

Your notes:_____

_____

_____

_____

#316 - CHANGE

Describe a single day or single incident that changed your life

- Birth of a child or grandchild

- Catastrophic accident, injury, or illness
- First date
- Death of a loved one
- A chance meeting
- A time when you were lucky
- Your wedding day
- Or?

Your notes:_____

_____

_____

_____

❧

"Hardship"
by Robert Hamer

After 45 years of marriage, ten children and fourteen hour work days, in 1935 my grandparents, Emma and William Brundle, were beginning to be rewarded. Their five surviving children had moved from the farm after World War I, and Will and Emma managed alone their eighty acres and a country store in rural Grape, Michigan.

One night a spark from the wood burning kitchen stove ignited the shingle roof. The building burned to the ground, destroying the store and attached living quarters. The only building to survive was the out-house. The two old people in their night clothes rescued each other, but no property was spared from the flames. My cousins and I later found a few pennies grossly bent by the heat, but everything else was gone.

Neighbors later described the red fireball that illuminated the night sky and the frantic efforts to save the property. The only fire truck was in Dundee, ten miles away. Everything burned: cherished photos of deceased children, furniture, store merchandise, truck, and heirlooms. What little cash Grandpa had accumulated was destroyed. Nothing survived and there was no insurance.

The Brundle conflagration was a tragic hardship, but Emma and Will recovered to celebrate their golden wedding anniversary. In my memory they were never cross with one another, never complained, and were never despondent. Their losses from the fire did not conquer my grandmother's humorous spirit or her loving authority over her husband, children, and grandchildren.

#317 - FIRE

<u>If your house was on fire and you had only five minutes to gather together some possessions and evacuate, what would you take?</u>

Your notes:_____

_____

_____

_____

#318 - HUNGER

<u>What are you hungry for right now?</u>

Your notes:_____

_____

_____

_____

#319 - WATCHING

Go to a public place - a mall or park, your local coffee place, an airport or train station - and sit for a while watching people.

Write a story about a person you watched
What is it about this person that caught your eye?
- Why are they there?
- What are they doing?
Is there anything about this person that reminds you of yourself?

Your notes:_____

_____

_____

_____

#320 - WITHOUT

What did you grow up without?
- Indoor plumbing
- Television
- A private telephone line
- Your own room
- Privacy
- Financial security
- A car
- Or?
How did you feel when you finally had this thing?

Your notes:_____

_____

_____

_____

#321 - BIRTHDAYS

Rather than adding more and more candles to your birthday cake as you grow older, here is a suggestion from M.B. Use only three candles: one for the past, one for the present, and one for the future.

<u>Write a birthday message</u>
* This does not have to be a <u>real</u> message you plan to send to someone.

<u>Some suggestions:</u>
* To a friend or family member about a birthday you celebrated or plan to celebrate
* To yourself about a birthday that was either celebrated or <u>not</u> celebrated in a way you wanted or anticipated
* Recollections of "milestone" birthdays: 16th, 21st, 40th, 50th, 60th
* What you plan to do on your next birthday
* Birthday wishes to someone special in your life
* Birthday wishes to someone you haven't said "Happy Birthday" to in a long time
* Birthday wishes to a deceased loved one

Your notes:_____

_____

_____

_____

HELPFUL HINT #38 - GET A COLORING BOOK

Coloring can be relaxing, free up your mind, and keep you from obsessing about difficulties you may be having with your writing. There are many places you can purchase coloring books with sophisticated designs that are both challenging and relaxing to color. When I was a kid, there was nothing better than being the proud owner of the giant orange box of 64 Crayola crayons. So, get yourself a coloring book and some crayons, paints, or colored pencils, and get started.

Our friend Susan F. suggested that you use the pages you color as chapter dividers in your autobiography. What a great idea!

#322 - YOUR BIRTHDAY

<u>What is the most memorable birthday you ever had?</u>
- The best birthday you ever had
- The worst birthday you ever had

<u>How has the way you celebrate your birthday changed as you've aged?</u>

Your notes:_____

_____

_____

_____

#323 - CURIOSITY

<u>What makes you curious?</u>

Your notes:_____

_____

_____

_____

#324 - MEANINGFUL

<u>What makes your life meaningful?</u>

Your notes:_____

_____

_____

_____

#325 - OLD CLOTHES

<u>Do you have a piece of old clothing you just can't seem to give up?</u>
- What is it about this piece of clothing that you love?

Your notes:_____

_____

_____

_____

#326 - EMBARRASSMENT

<u>Describe your most embarrassing moment</u>
- In childhood
- As an adult

Your notes:_____

_____

_____

_____

#327 - DON'T LIKE THAT PERSON

<u>Describe</u>
- The dullest person you ever met
- The meanest person you ever met
- The cruelest person you ever met

Your notes:_____

_____

_____

_____

HELPFUL HINT #39 - DATE WHAT YOU WRITE

Not only do you want to accurately date the events from your past, you also want to note the date on which you write down your stories. Your life changes as you change, and by dating what you write, you will know how you felt during a particular time of your life.

#328 - NO (1)

<u>Write about a time when you said no</u>

Your notes:_____

_____

_____

_____

#329 - NO (2)

<u>Write about a time when someone told you no</u>

Your notes:_____

_____

_____

_____

#330 - PERMISSION

<u>Describe a situation in which you acted without first obtaining permission</u>
- Did you later have to ask for forgiveness?

Your notes:_____

_____

_____

_____

#331 - BETTER (1)

<u>How are you making the world a better place?</u>
- Why does it matter that you are here?

Your notes:_____

_____

_____

_____

#332 - BETTER (2)

<u>How could you have done things better?</u>
- "I could have been a better son or daughter or mother or father or sister or brother or friend or employee if I had only … "

Your notes:_____

_____

_____

_____

SIXTEEN

HELPFUL HINT #40 - ACKNOWLEDGE, ATONE, APOLOGIZE

Mom and I have been teaching our autobiography class for a while now, but we're always open to new ideas, and so a few months ago we took a memoir writing class. During a discussion with the instructor, I mentioned two best-selling contemporary memoirs I had read and absolutely hated. I disliked the narrator of the first book because she expressed no guilt and offered no apologies for participating in the international drug trade. I disliked the narrator of the second book because she apparently found it acceptable that she and her brother first starved and then murdered their deceased mother's beloved horse.

I would have liked these authors so much better and not disliked their books so much if at some point they had apologized and expressed some remorse. I asked the instructor if she thought that atonement was a necessary part of memoir writing. She said perhaps not atonement, but certainly acknowledgement.

We all make mistakes and hurt others, whether intentionally or accidentally. I am not a therapist nor a pastor, and I don't know if you need to apologize to those you've hurt for the good of your soul. That is an issue far beyond the scope of this book. But maybe you have to at least admit your mistakes to yourself and take personal responsibility for the unkind things you've done.

Acknowledge. Atone. Apologize. Then decide what to do with it. File it away. Include it in your memoir. Give it to the person you hurt. Perform some sort of cleansing ritual. And then move on and forgive yourself for being human.

#333 - KNOWING

<u>What do you know?</u>

Your notes:_____

_____

_____

_____

#334 - TRUST

<u>Who do you trust?</u>

Your notes:_____

_____

_____

_____

#335 - LESS TRAVELED

In his poem "The Road Not Taken", Robert Frost wrote, "I took the one less traveled by, and that has made all the difference."

<u>When and how have you taken the road less traveled?</u>
- How has it make a difference?

- What were the positive and negative impacts of your decision?

Was there a time when you did not take the road less traveled? Why not?

- You weren't brave enough
- You did what was expected, rather than what you wanted
- Or?

How did *not* taking the road less traveled make a difference?

- What were the positive and negative impacts of your decision?

Your notes:_____

_____

_____

_____

#336 - DISASTER

Write about a natural disaster that changed your life

- Tornado
- Earthquake
- Fire
- Flood
- Drought
- Storm
- Monsoon, tropical storm, or hurricane
- Lightening strike

What happened?

- Loss of life
- Loss of residence
- Loss of other property
- Loss of lifestyle
- Loss of livelihood
- Or?

What did you do to recover?

Your notes:_____

_____

_____

_____

#337 - IMMINENT

<u>Have you ever been near death?</u>
<u>What happened to make you believe you were facing imminent death?</u>
- Illness
- Injury
- Suicidal thoughts

<u>Was this an irrational fear or were you actually near death?</u>
- How were you able to survive?

<u>Did other people think you were near death?</u>

Your notes:_____

_____

_____

_____

HELPFUL HINT #41 - IT'S NOT SCHOOL

Feeling a bit overwhelmed? Remember, this is <u>**NOT**</u> school and you do not need to answer everything!

#338 - PRIVATE

<u>Where do you find your privacy?</u>
- Is having privacy important to you?

Your notes:_____

_____

_____

_____

#339 - YOU AS A GRANDPARENT

Use this exercise to also write about your great-grandchildren.

<u>What do your grandchildren call you?</u>
- Oma
- Granny
- Gramps
- Nana
- Grandma or Grandpa
- Abba
- GG (for Great-Grand)
- Or?

<u>What are the names of your grandchildren?</u>
<u>Who are the parents of your grandchildren?</u>
- Who do your grandchildren resemble?

Write about the birth of each of your grandchildren
- How you heard about the pregnancy
- How you heard about the birth
- The first time you saw and held each of your grandchildren

When do you see your grandchildren?
- Regularly because they live with you, visit often, or you babysit
- Holidays and other special occasions
- Weekly family dinners
- At worship services
- Not often because they live too far away
- Not often due to an estrangement

Describe the special things you do with your grandchildren
- How has your relationship with your grandchildren changed as they've aged?

What treasures have you saved to give to your grandchildren?

Your notes:_____

_____

_____

_____

#340 - RECIPE

Do you have a special or favorite family recipe?
Is there a story or tradition behind this recipe?
- Family recipe handed down from generation to generation
- The dish always served on special occasions or holidays
- A recipe you invented
- A family or traditional recipe you adapted to your family's tastes

What is this recipe?
- Ingredients and directions

Your notes:_____

_____

_____

_____

#341 - DOG / CAT

<u>What does your dog or cat know about you?</u>
- What do you do in secret that only your dog or cat sees?

Your notes:_____

_____

_____

_____

#342 - SMELL

Experts say your sense of smell is the most evocative of your senses, and the one most likely to trigger memories.

<u>Go smell something, and write about the memories it brings to mind</u>

Your notes:_____

_____

_____

_____

#343 - CONCERT

<u>Write about the first concert you attended</u>
- Name of the performer(s)
- Venue

<u>Who went with you?</u>

<u>Is there any aspect of the performance you remember?</u>
- A particular song
- Light show or dance

<u>Did you have a personal encounter with the performer(s) after the concert?</u>

Your notes:_____

_____

_____

_____

#344 - HISTORY

<u>Describe the actions taken by you or your parents in response to a historical event or social trend</u>
- Economic downturn or depression
- War
- Changes in government
- Epidemic
- Natural disaster
- Economic upturn or boom
- The Space Race
- The Jazz Age / Roaring Twenties
- Terrorism
- Shift in population from farm to city
- The technological age
- Or?

Your notes:_____

_____

_____

_____

#345 - CURRENT INTERESTS

<u>What are you interested in right now?</u>
- Studying a particular historical event or era
- A person
- Religion
- Health
- Retirement
- New career
- New recipes
- Learning a new skill
- Pursuing an old skill
- Finding old friends
- Something you said you'd do if you had the time
- Creating art
- Caring for a loved one
- Or?

Your notes:_____

_____

_____

_____

HELPFUL HINT #42 - OLD LETTERS

Go through any old letters you've saved, and use them to help you remember what you were doing and what was important to you during certain periods of your life. Ask your friends and family if they saved any letters from you, and if you can take a look at them. Quote from these old letters and weave them into the story of your life.

#346 - ACTIVISM

<u>Have you ever been an activist?</u>
- Anti-war
- Peace Corps
- Gun control issues
- Women, racial, LGBT rights
- Workers' rights
- Religious issues
- Environmental issues
- Consumer protection
- Politics

<u>Describe your activism</u>
- Marches
- Rallies
- Grass roots campaigning
- Petitioning
- Letter writing
- Public speaking
- Fundraising
- Or?

Your notes:_____

_____

_____

_____

#347 - CHARMING

<u>Describe the most charming person you ever met</u>
- What was it about this person that was so charming?

<u>Do you consider yourself to be a charming person?</u>

Your notes:_____

_____

_____

_____

❧

"Prince Charming"
by Christine Jeston

It was May 27, 1979. I was in my second year at the National Institute of Dramatic Arts in Sydney, and thinking what a beautiful crisp autumn day it was as I rode the bus from Paddington to Kensington. When I walked out of my voice class at NIDA James Belton, a fellow student, ran up and wished me a happy birthday. Surprise! He told me he was going to take me to town to see the Queen for my birthday.

Queen Elizabeth II was opening the Eastern Suburbs Railway that morning. James had always been a Royalist and was proud of it. He was so brave, admitting it without caring what anyone thought. Believe me, there were plenty of people who thought we should have our independence from Britain, and resented Australia footing any royal bills.

James and I met our first day at NIDA. How could I not fall in love with this gorgeous man? The first words out of his mouth were, "I am so nervous because I thought everyone would be much older than me. I am so glad to meet someone my own age. My name is James, what's yours?" He had me! He was 17 years old and I, a 24 year old married lady, but I didn't want to say anything as I didn't want to burst his bubble. We were best friends from that day on, and have remained close ever since. James was extremely good looking and a very nice person. He had a beautiful voice you could listen to forever and proved to be an excellent actor. I never understood his lack of confidence. Because he could not hack the uncertainty of the business, he gave up acting to be a Qantas flight attendant, despite having success in a couple of films and TV shows and having one of the top agents.

Let's get back to my 26th birthday surprise. James couldn't wait to get started, so we walked down to Anzac Parade to catch a bus to Martin Place where the Queen was going to head after the opening ceremony at Bondi Junction. She was going to walk out of the tunnel and past the post office to George Street and her motorcade. When we got there, only a few people were congregating, so we sat on the ground and chatted until we saw some men starting to put up barricades. We asked a police woman if she knew which side the Queen would be walking down and she told us the left side, so we positioned ourselves and settled in for the wait.

After a long time, a bunch of men in grey suits started to come out of the tunnel talking on their headphones and doing whatever the Secret Intelligence Service people do, when we saw the Queen way over on the other side. We knew it was her because we spied her hat first. Everyone got excited and some people started cheering. I found myself getting caught up in all the hoopla and was very put out because I couldn't get a good look at her. As I was up on my tippy toes and stretching my neck to get a peek, several men on the other side of the railing were blocking my view so I said very loudly, "Would you please get out of the way. I want to see the Queen!" One of the men looked me straight in the eye and said in the most beautiful English accent, "I am terribly sorry, you'll just have to put up with me."

I had to take a breath as I was utterly bowled over by this gentlemen's grace and charisma. I had insulted Royalty! He was Prince Phillip, the Duke of Edinburgh. The Queen's better half, but after seeing him I would definitely say he just may be the better half of that union. Wow!

I have never found the Duke to be particularly handsome or striking, but this man had an unmistakable presence. He was so charming. It washed through me before I realized who he was, and I completely forgot about Her Majesty. I looked at James horrified. He said, "Bubby, this is one birthday you'll never forget."

If this had happened two hundred years before, I may have found myself in the Tower of London or shipped off to the colonies. Oh yes, I was already there, but you get my drift. He really had the most captivating smile and I would say sense of humor. I guess you would have to have one if you always had to walk behind your wife.

Just what is charisma? You always know if someone possesses it. CocoB my Maltese has it. I have heard the Dali Lama has it, and I am sure George Clooney has it although I have never met him. The Bible says that Jesus had an unmistakable presence. This list is not necessarily in order. Don't judge me - although I do think my dog should stay at the top of the list.

Take my word for it, the Duke has <u>it</u>. I have no idea if Liz has it or not as I never had the privilege, but you never know what will happen. I never imagined when I woke up on my 26th birthday in 1979, that by the end of the day I would have insulted Royalty.

#348 - MIRROR

<u>What do you see when you look in a mirror?</u>

Your notes:_____

_____

_____

_____

#349 - TROUBLE

<u>Describe the most trouble you've ever been in</u>

Your notes:_____

_____

_____

_____

#350 - TIME CAPSULE

<u>What item(s) would you put in a time capsule?</u>
- The item(s) may be personal to you or something else
- Choose something representative of the present time

<u>Write a letter accompanying your item(s) to be read when the time capsule is opened in 100 years</u>
- Describe why you selected the item(s)
- How the item(s) are representative of life in the present time

Your notes:_____

_____

_____

_____

#351 - SAY

<u>What is it that you just can't seem to say?</u>

Your notes:_____

_____

_____

_____

#352 - ABUNDANCE

How can you achieve abundance?
What gives you feelings of abundance?

Your notes:_____

_____

_____

_____

SEVENTEEN

"Writing is easy. You just cross out the wrong words."

- MARK TWAIN -

HELPFUL HINT #43 - GET UNSTUCK

If you are absolutely stuck, try writing a letter, a thank you note, or a prayer. The important thing is to start writing!!

❈

#353 - ISOLATION

<u>Describe a time when you were isolated or felt isolated</u>

Your notes:_____

_____

_____

_____

#354 - SURPRISE (1)

<u>What do people not know about you that may surprise them?</u>

Your notes:_____

_____

_____

_____

#355 - SURPRISE (2)

<u>Write about a time when you were surprised</u>

Your notes:_____

_____

_____

_____

#356 - LOSS OF A TREASURED THING

<u>Was anything you treasured ever lost or destroyed? How?</u>
- A physical object
- Something intangible such as loss of a friendship

<u>Were you able to re-create or regain this thing or was it lost forever?</u>
- Was the re-created or regained thing better or worse than the original?

<u>How did the loss change you?</u>
- How did you recover from your loss?
- Did you forgive the person who caused the loss?

Your notes:_____

_____

_____

_____

❧

"Loss of Something Treasured"
by Sallie Ringle

It's 26 years now. This loss has cut into me deeply. You see my loss is of my brother. He did not die. He stopped having a relationship with me. For over 20 years he has refused to speak to me. I was never allowed a relationship with my nephews, and knew only what my mother shared with me. This was especially hard for me because my brother is my only sibling.

I will explain the circumstances which brought about this loss. In the fall of 1989, I got a call from my brother in Maine asking if I would be willing to look after his wife's great-uncle if they sent him down to Florida for the winter. At the time I was working cleaning houses, helping some elderly manage their homes, going to college, and taking care of my own family. But I said, "Yes of course." Uncle Ozzie would pay me a small amount for my trouble.

Uncle Ozzie was to stay at a motel with long-term stay accommodations. He would need me to take him grocery shopping, do his laundry, and check up on him. I found him to be completely delightful. He had a few strange behaviors, but I figured they were because he was born in 1900.

I really involved Uncle Ozzie in our family life. I would bring him home for dinner. He and I would go on little adventures together. As a family we took him to church with us occasionally. Uncle Ozzie would ask me why I was so good to him, and I replied that I really liked him and that it was my Christian obligation to serve others.

In the spring of 1990, his niece came down from Maine and stayed for a week. Uncle Ozzie got sick after she left and was hospitalized. I realized he was not well enough to go back to his motel apartment, and brought him to live with my family. He was with us for six weeks before I was to fly him back to Maine. Now you need to understand that Uncle Ozzie was very much intact mentally. He was on constant oxygen and a special diet which I followed rigorously plus a boatload of medicine which I managed.

The end of May it was arranged for me to fly him home to Maine. I made arrangements to have an oxygen machine delivered to the hotel in Bangor so it would be there when we arrived. I was concerned that he would not have oxygen while we were actually traveling, but he was OK.

However, there was a little catch. In one of the phone calls Uncle Ozzie made from my house, he had made arrangements for his New York lawyer to meet him in Bangor. I knew nothing about this until we were at the hotel and he told me. He made me promise not to tell on him because his family wouldn't let him talk to his lawyer, and this was the only way he could do it. After I had seen how his niece treated him the week she was in Florida, I believed him. I stayed away while the consultations were going on between Uncle Ozzie and his lawyer.

The family found out about this meeting when they arrived in Bangor. They were hopping mad. My sister-in-law yelled at me. Her mother was furious and accused me of all sorts of ugly things. The truth was I knew nothing about what went on with the lawyer. The six days I spent in Maine with my brother and his family were some of the worst days of my life.

About a month after I got home, I got a call from my father saying he was coming to see me and had something important to discuss. Dad lived in California and I was in Florida, and I couldn't imagine what was so important he would fly all the way out to see me.

Well, it was important. Seems Uncle Ozzie had died about ten days after I took him home. When he met with his lawyer, he had changed his will. He had taken out an inheritance to a deceased niece's husband. The money that was to go to this man was now to go to me. I knew nothing of this. That started the family feud. My brothers-in-law sued me and I had to go to New York City to appear at trial. The first day of the trial the judge threatened my brother's family with jail for tampering with the mail. They had opened Uncle Ozzie's mail from the law office and found out what he had done. In the end the judge told the lawyers to make a settlement and not come back to court until it was finalized.

I agreed to settle for half of the amount left to me. The lawyer would get a third of that. In the end it wasn't enough to have lost my only brother over. It is said that there are no wars worse than families fighting over money. I have found that to be so true. I know that I am innocent of having any part in the changes *to the will. I think Uncle Ozzie was so happy and thankful for what I did for him that he wanted to do this for me. If I had known what he was doing I might have told him that he shouldn't include me in his will.*

About five years ago my brother started to talk to me because our mother began failing. He will only talk to me about her. He has come to California several times and is cordial, but not caring or loving. That part of our lives is dead. It makes me so sad. I know that once Mother dies I will never have contact with my brother again. This is a loss I will never got over.

#357 - MEALS

<u>What is the best meal you ever ate?</u>
- What made it the best?

<u>What is the worst or most disappointing meal you ever ate?</u>
- What made it so bad?

Your notes:_____

_____

_____

_____

#358 - COOKING (1)

<u>What was the first thing you learned to cook?</u>
- Who taught you?

Your notes:_____

_____

_____

_____

#359 - COOKING (2)

<u>What was your favorite thing your mother made?</u>
- If you have the recipe, write it down to share with family members

<u>What was your least favorite thing your mother made?</u>

Your notes:_____

_____

_____

_____

#360 - PRAYER

<u>Write a prayer</u>

Your notes:_____

_____

_____

_____

#361 - EXPLANATION

<u>Write a letter explaining yourself to someone you have not seen in a long time</u>

Your notes:_____

_____

_____

_____

"Writing is a lot of erasing. You can't edit a blank page."

- PENNY GUISINGER -

HELPFUL HINT #44 - DON'T BE AFRAID OF REWRITING

Don't be afraid of first drafts, second drafts, and third drafts. Write and rewrite and write again until your story is told the way you want to tell it. Then you have to let your baby go, and get some feedback. After drafting and redrafting, you lose your perspective and can no longer view your work objectively. At that point, it's time to call in someone else to give you a fresh viewpoint.

#362 - OTHER PEOPLE

<u>If you could meet anyone – historical figure, celebrity, ancestor - either living or dead – who would you meet and what would you say?</u>
- Why did you choose this person?
- What would you ask this person?

Your notes:_____

_____

_____

_____

#363 - *CARPE DIEM*

<u>What do you do to seize the day?</u>

Your notes:_____

_____

_____

_____

#364 - ADMIRATION

<u>Write a letter to a living person you admire</u>
- Tell this person why you admire him or her

<u>Will you mail this letter?</u>

Your notes:_____

_____

_____

_____

#365 - LONG

"Think long thoughts."

- P.D. OUSPENSKY -

<u>What are your long thoughts?</u>

Your notes:_____

_____

_____

_____

❧

"Writing Workshop: Day One"
by Barbara Cauthorn

What is this? It's a big room and a small group of people. We're seated around three long tables, put together into a square. The chairs are comfortable, padded with an attractive red fabric. This is a writing workshop. What am I doing here? I drove over 1,000 miles for this? What is wrong with me? Obviously, everyone else is busy writing, thinking, concentrating and creating interesting stuff. Look at the intensity on their faces. I have nothing to say.

The room is stuffy, without fans or air conditioning The shades are drawn to keep out the hot July sun. They are not accustomed to hot July sun here in northern Maine. There is a dream-catcher hanging on the wall over the fire extinguisher, next to the door marked EXIT. Is this a metaphor for something? Will all dreams be caught before you reach the exit sign?

I take another sip of cold coffee. I can't possibly do this. All my dreams must be stuck in that damned dream catcher.

I read this morning that you should "just keep your hand moving" during writing practice. OK. My hand is moving and there are words on the paper. But they're meaningless garbage. There is no one at my side offering ideas; no ethereal guide appearing in an enlightened corner of my brain with clever words or good ideas. Nothing. Nada. Zilch. Empty.

When is lunch? Is it soon? I know how to eat lunch. I don't know how to do this.

#366 - TO FORGET

What are the painful memories you just can't seem to forget?
- Hurtful treatment by another person
- Hurtful comments by another person
- Death or permanent loss of a person or relationship
- Something hurtful you said or did to another person
- Or?

If you could free yourself from these memories, what would change?
- How you feel about yourself or another person
- Your attitude toward life
- It would make no difference

Since the past cannot be changed, how have you learned to live with these memories?
- Do you need to forgive yourself or others?

Your notes:_____

_____

_____

_____

#367 - JEWELRY

Do you have a special piece of jewelry?
What is the significance of this piece?
- Wedding or engagement ring
- Class ring
- First piece of "real" jewelry you owned
- Family heirloom

- Gift from a special person

<u>When do you wear this piece of jewelry?</u>

- Everyday
- On special occasions
- Never - It's too valuable, too old-fashioned, or locked in a safety deposit box

<u>Who will receive this piece of jewelry when you are gone?</u>

Your notes:_____

_____

_____

_____

#368 - SIMPLE

"If you can't explain something simply, you don't really understand it."

- BILL GATES -

❧

<u>Explain something simply that you know how to do very well</u>

Your notes:_____

_____

_____

_____

#369 - BRAVERY

<u>When have you been brave?</u>
- Physical bravery
- Speaking up in support of someone or something unpopular
- Demonstrating the courage of your convictions
- Standing up to a bully

<u>Did you ever speak up or take action when you saw something wrong?</u>
- What did you say?
- What was the result?

Your notes:_____

_____

_____

_____

#370 - STRONG (1)

<u>How are you strong?</u>
- Physically strong
- Mentally strong
- Emotionally strong
- Spiritually strong

Your notes:_____

_____

_____

_____

#371 - STRONG (2)

<u>Who is the strongest person in your family?</u>
- What does this person do to demonstrate strength?

<u>How are you like this person?</u>

Your notes:_____

_____

_____

_____

❈

"The Intruder"
by Lynda Barr

It saddens me to realize that it sometimes takes the threat of losing your child to remind you just how precious their life is to you. In January, 1989 my 17 year old son Jeff had just started living with his dad in Chino, and my 15 year old daughter Robin was living with me. While I was working the 3:00 p.m. to 11:00 p.m. shift at IOLAB Corp in Claremont, I received a very sobering call from an Upland police officer. He told me that my house had been broken into and my daughter was OK but very upset. He wanted me to come home as soon as I could. I immediately felt panicky, but tried to keep myself calm so I could drive the four miles home without getting a speeding ticket or into an accident.

When I came into my house, several policemen and a large German shepherd dog were there. One of the policemen was questioning my daughter who was shaking uncontrollably and crying. Robin's next words were, "He then came into my bedroom and sat down on my back with a leg on each side of me and that's when I started screaming." When I heard her words my mouth fell open and visions of my mother-in-law being murdered by the Night Stalker just three years earlier painfully entered my mind!

I knew full well that I could have lost my child if the intruder had the same malicious intentions as my mother-in-law's intruder had. Suddenly I welcomed my daughter's crying and shaking. It was living proof that she was still very much alive. I vowed then that no other person would again violate the privacy of our home or terrorize my daughter! With money that my work lent me, I secured the house with new locks, security lights, and a peek hole in the front door.

Robin and I became a lot closer and much more concerned about each other's safety and welfare, especially when we knew that one of us would be home alone. I thanked God everyday that I still had a daughter who I could love, hug, and share my life with. Robin, who is now 43, and her husband Mike now have two daughters of their own. And life continues on ...

#372 - ELECTIONS

<u>What is the first US Presidential election in which you voted?</u>
- For whom did you vote?
- Why?

<u>Did you work on the campaign?</u>

Your notes:_____

_____

_____

_____

#373 - COLOR

<u>Write about a color</u>
<u>A color may remind you of many things</u>
- A favorite outfit
- A room
- Food

- Something in nature, i.e. a sunset, a forest, an animal
- An emotion
- A person
- Or?

<u>What do you like or dislike about this color?</u>

Your notes:_____

_____

_____

_____

#374 - OUTDOORS

<u>Write your memories of the "great outdoors"</u>
- What is the most beautiful thing in nature you have ever seen?

Your notes:_____

_____

_____

_____

#375 - YOU CAN'T PLEASE EVERYONE

<u>Have you ever felt someone just did not like you?</u>
- How did that make you feel?

<u>Did you do things to get this person to like you?</u>
- Were your efforts successful?
- Did this person ever like you?

<u>What, if any, negative impacts were caused by this person's dislike of you?</u>
- Employer or boss who did not like you
- Teacher who did not like you

- Club president or advisor who did not like you
- Relative who did not like you

<u>If you were not able to become friends with this person, how did you deal with the rejection?</u>

Your notes:_____

_____

_____

_____

HELPFUL HINT #45 - KEEP 'EM GUESSING

It is important that you capture your readers' attention with the first few sentences. You are not writing a school essay, so stay away from formal introductions that slow the pace of your story. You want to engage your readers by *telling* your story, not *explaining* it.

You also want your readers to keep reading, so don't give away your story in the first few paragraphs. Hold a few things back and don't strip yourself bare in the first paragraph. Use the unexpected word or phrase to leave your readers guessing so they want to come back for more.

#376 - ACCOMPLISHMENT

<u>Other people may find this easy, but it was not for me, and when I did it, it was a real accomplishment</u>
<u>Here are some suggestions:</u>

- Cooked a gourmet meal
- Baked a cake

- Fixed a computer problem
- Took a solo trip
- Chaired a committee
- Spoke in public
- Rode a horse
- Swam in the ocean
- Took a hike
- Asked for a raise
- Sang in public
- Or?

Your notes:_____

_____

_____

_____

#377 - NEW REALITY

Sometimes things happen that change your reality. You go from being a spouse to a widow. You go from being healthy and fit to a person with physical challenges. You go from employed to unemployed, or financially secure to insolvent.

How did you deal with your new reality?
- What changes did you make?
Was the change expected or unexpected?
Have things improved for you?

Your notes:_____

_____

_____

_____

#378 - SMARTER

What do you know now that you wish you had known back then?
- If you had known it back then, would it have made a difference?

Your notes:_____

_____

_____

_____

#379 - IMPORTANT PERSON

Find a photo of someone important to you.

Why is this person important to you?
Describe when and where the photo was taken
- What are your memories of that day?

Your notes:_____

_____

_____

_____

#380 - RESOLUTION

It doesn't need to be New Year's for you to make a resolution. Make one
How will you work on accomplishing the resolution you just made?
- Do you think you'll be able to do it?

What are your usual resolutions?
- Lose weight
- Quit smoking

- Exercise
- Save money
- Get a new job
- Fall in love
- Or?

Your notes:_____

_____

_____

_____

EIGHTEEN

HELPFUL HINT #46 - HONOR OTHERS

Telling your story gives you a chance to honor others, because your story is also the story of your family and your friends. Telling your story honors others as it honors you.

#381 - DANGEROUS

<u>What is the most physically dangerous thing you have ever done?</u>
- What made you decide to take this risk?
- How did it make you feel to take this risk?
- Were you hurt?
- What was the outcome?

Your notes:_____

_____

_____

_____

#382 - TIME

<u>How are you about time?</u>
- Always late
- Always early

<u>Was there a time when being late or being early had a major impact on you, either positively or negatively?</u>
- You missed an opportunity because you were too late
- You were first in line because you were early

Your notes:_____

_____

_____

_____

#383 - HALF-GLASS

<u>Is your glass half-empty or half-full?</u>
- Why do you have this outlook?

Your notes:_____

_____

_____

_____

#384 - ADVERSITY

<u>What did you accomplish in the face of adversity?</u>

Your notes:_____

_____

_____

_____

#385 - WAR

Your memories and thoughts of war are truly of your time and place. My mother's memories are of the "good" war - World War Two - and her work in an aircraft factory assembling planes for combat. My memories are of a different time and a different war. Although I am a Baby Boomer and remember my brothers playing "war" games, my own memories are of Vietnam and anti-war protests. You may have memories of the return from war of a parent you had not seen for years, or family stories and memories of incarceration in internment or concentration camps. If you have no memories of war, feel blessed that you have lived your life in peace, and move on to the next topic.

Which war is "your" war?
Write about your war memories
- Military service
- Branch and rank
- Combat

Did you earn any medals or commendations?
- Describe the action for which you earned your citation

Were you injured?
- Describe how you were injured

What memories do you have of your "comrades in arms?"
What impact did your military service have on your later life?
- Benefits provided under the GI Bill
- Where you chose to live after your service
- Post-war career choices
- A change in your basic attitudes and philosophy of life
- On-going effects from a wound or post-traumatic stress
- What was it like to return to civilian life?

How did the military service of a family member have an impact on your life?
Were you in support services?
Were you an anti-war protester?

Your notes:_____

_____

_____

_____

❧

"How Our Family Survived the War"
by Joy Karsevar
told in the voice of her father
Ricardo Tomacruz

I was barely 17 when World War II broke out in the Philippines. We heard news of the Japanese attack on Pearl Harbor over the radio. Due to the time difference, we heard on Monday morning, and I was in school. We were having a flag ceremony. I remember there were two flags - the Philippine flag and the American flag. The Philippines was then a Commonwealth of the United States. An announcement came from the school authorities, "NO SCHOOL!" We all cheered! HOORAY!! Little did we realize it would be the last time we would be in high school, and there would be no school for four years.

Life changed instantly. The Japanese bombed Manila. There was death, chaos, and evacuations every-where. The Japanese put up sentry posts where we had to line up, bow to them, and get checked. I can still hear them shouting, KORA, KORA, KORA!" meaning, "LISTEN!" They would slap anyone who did not fall in line or bow to them. Our once upper class lifestyle changed overnight. It was war time. Our cars and properties were confiscated. We were down to only being able to put food on the table and stay alive.

When the Japanese bombed our city on Christmas Day, our family decided it was time to evacuate. We moved south to Hagonoy province, and later to Manila. There were more killings and torture at the whim of the Japanese army. Our house in Cabanatuan was occupied by Japanese nurses without our knowledge or permission. They made it their home for the duration of the war.

My father converted our wagon-car into a pick-up van to avoid ambushes. It ran on alcohol since there was no gasoline. We had to apply for alcohol, and there was a ration of 100 liters for three months. A hundred liters was good for only one round trip from Manila to Cabanatuan, and we needed to transport rice. My 19 year old brother Louie would apply for alcohol and show a business card he had from a pre-war Japanese friend of my dad who was a Colonel in the Japanese army. Before the war the Colonel and my dad did business, and he became a good friend. His card helped us get a double ration of alcohol, and again later in a way we never could have imagined.

During the war we lived in fear and suffering, never knowing when the next bombing and Japanese attacks would happen. We had to be continuously alert and ready to go to the bunkers to shelter from the bombs. Nothing was stable. We had to be ready to evacuate at a moment's notice.

In the last six months of the war, my family decided to go back to our province because we had no more food in Manila. Things were all right for a while, although a lot of the locals told us not to stay since there were fierce Japanese soldiers in the area, but we did not listen. We were just too lax.

One day my mom and Louie were hanging white sheets outside on the laundry line. The Japanese saw this and thought they were giving signals to the American fighter planes. They came to our house and arrested my dad and my brother and accused them of helping the Americans. My mom, the rest of my siblings, and I were not arrested, and to this day I do not know why.

They brought my dad to a field, and were ready to kill him, when luckily he remembered the business card of his Japanese Colonel friend. His friend had said, "Show my card when it is a matter of life and death." He showed it to his Japanese captors, and they were impressed my dad knew the Colonel since he was a respected and high ranking officer. They drove my brother Louie far away from us, and we really thought they would kill him. We were so sad and thought we would never see him again. We were shocked to see him walking home 24 hours later. We asked what made them release him. He said that when he was in the vehicle he started talking with a Japanese officer who spoke good English, who was so impressed with Louie that he felt compassion and released him.

We felt so happy. We were ecstatic when the <u>next</u> <u>day</u> the Japanese surrendered and the war was over. Our family of ten was so blessed not to have had a single prisoner or casualty of war.

⚜

#386 - FUN

<u>What do you do for fun?</u>
- How do you feel when you are unable to do these fun things?

Your notes:_____

_____

_____

_____

#387 - I KNEW

<u>I knew I was getting older when . . .</u>

Your notes:_____

_____

_____

_____

#388 - SPRINGTIME

<u>For many people spring is a time of new beginnings. Write about spring</u>
<u>Here are some suggestions:</u>
- Memories of past Easter, Passover, Solstice, Holaka, or other spring celebrations
- Coloring Easter eggs

- Peeps and other Easter candy
- Spring break from school
- Melting snow and the "mud" season
- Sowing crops and the birth of farm animals
- Sunshine after winter's darkness
- Daylight Savings Time

What do you like about spring?
What do you dislike about spring?

Your notes:_____
_____
_____
_____

#389 - DESTINY

Do you (or did you) believe you had a destiny or special purpose?
- Did you fulfill your destiny?

If you have not yet fulfilled your destiny, are you still working on fulfilling it?
- What are you doing?

Your notes:_____
_____
_____
_____

#390 - DISAPPOINTMENT

Describe a disappointment you experienced as a child
- You didn't get the part
- You didn't get the A

- You didn't make the squad
- You didn't make the team
- You weren't asked to the dance
- You lost an election
- You realized there was no Santa
- You weren't allowed to do something you really wanted to do
- Or?

Your notes:_____

_____

_____

_____

❧

"Teeth"
by Robert Hamer

As a child, my twice a year visits to the dentist were as regular as the vernal and autumnal equinox. After one visit and just before leaving, the dentist handed me a package of Wrigley's Juicy Fruit gum and said, "Chew lots of this."

He may have included admonitions regarding time, place, and frequency, but these niceties were lost on me. And so chew I did. From the end of the dental appointment until dinner, and from after dinner until bedtime, I chewed and chewed and chewed.

At junior high the next morning, I told the instructor my dentist's professional advice, citing it as giving me the authority to break the rule against gum chewing in class. My teacher stood with his arms folded, looking down at me. He glared at me, wilting my confidence in the doctor's orders. Finally, he shifted his weight, unfolded his arms, put his hands in his pockets, heaved an exasperated sigh and asked, "How many hours in a day?"

"Twenty-four," I responded.

"How many hours do you sleep?"

"Eight."

"How many does that leave?"

"Sixteen."

"How many hours are you in school"

"Seven."

"How many hours does that leave?"

"Nine."

"Don't you think," he said, "that chewing gum nine hours a day is just about all that your dentist can expect?"

❈

#391 - VALUES

What are your most deeply held values?
- What values are an integral part of who you are?

Was there ever a time when your values were challenged?
- How did you respond to this challenge?
- Did your values waver?

Have your most deeply held values changed as you've aged?

Your notes:_____

_____

_____

_____

❦

HELPFUL HINT #47 - USE A DISGUISE

There may be situations in which you want to protect the privacy or identity of another person. You can do this by creating a disguise. Use false names or change the date or location of the event you are describing.

❦

#392 - DEAR CHILD

<u>Write a letter to the youngest member of your family</u>
- What wisdom do you want to share?
- What do you have to say to welcome this child to your family?

Your notes:_____

_____

_____

_____

#393 - CONCEPTS OF OLD AGE

<u>What was your concept of "old age" when you were a child?</u>
- How old did a person have to be to be considered "old"?

<u>How has your idea of old age changed as you've aged?</u>
- What age do you now consider old?

<u>What age do you feel now?</u>
- What age do you look?

Your notes:_____

_____

_____

_____

#394 - PROTECTION

<u>How do you protect yourself?</u>

Your notes:_____

_____

_____

_____

#395 - POLITE

<u>How are you polite?</u>
- When are you polite?

<u>Was there a time when being impolite was your only choice?</u>
- Why?

Your notes:_____

_____

_____

_____

#396 - HOLIDAY LETTER

Many people have a tradition of sending annual holiday letters summing up the past year's events. The story of your life is not just what happened to you many years ago, it is also what happened to you recently. Even if you do not mail this letter, it is a good way to look back on the year and record the recent events in your life.

<u>Write a holiday letter</u>
- Think about what you did during the past year: people and places visited, illness survived, birth and loss, new things you tried, plays you saw, books you read, whatever made up the fabric of your life during the year
- Write about it

Your notes:_____

_____

_____

_____

#397 - YEAR END (2)

<u>What does the end of the year mean to you?</u>
- Holidays
- Returning to school in the fall
- College football
- The changing of seasons and the coming of winter
- The first celebration of a year-end holiday you remember

- The first year-end holiday after the loss of a loved one
- Fall and winter activities - skiing, ice skating, shoveling snow (or summer activities if you live in the Southern Hemisphere)
- Or?

Your notes:_____

_____

_____

_____

HELPFUL HINT #48 - LET ANOTHER PERSON READ YOUR DRAFT

Before you commit to publishing your book, have another person read your final draft. When you read your own work over and over again there will be errors you just don't see.

Your reader should be someone you trust to provide honest feedback.

#398 - FORGIVENESS

<u>What actions have you taken for which you cannot seem to forgive yourself?</u>
- What can you do to forgive yourself?

<u>How has the inability to forgive yourself impacted your life?</u>
- Does it continue to do so?

Your notes:_____

_____

_____

_____

#399 - LOVE THIS

Describe the thing you most love to do
- Activity or Sport
- Hobby (knitting, scrapbooking, stamp collecting, arts and crafts, etc.)
- A place you like to go (theater, out to dinner with friends, movies, etc.)
- Learning new things
- Or?

Why do you love doing this thing?

Your notes:_____

_____

_____

_____

#400 - BAD HABIT

How have you broken a bad habit?
- Quit smoking, drinking, overeating
- Overcome compulsions
- Conquered self-destructive behaviors

Your notes:_____

_____

_____

_____

#401 - LENGTH OF DAYS

<u>Do you find that your days are too short to accomplish all you want to do, or are your days too long to fill?</u>
*   What makes your days either too short or too long?
<u>Do you want your days to be filled with activity, or would you rather "stop and smell the roses"?</u>

Your notes:_____

_____

_____

_____

#402 - QUOTE

<u>What is your favorite quote?</u>
*   Why is it your favorite?

Your notes:_____

_____

_____

_____

#403 - BEYOND

What pain do you have that is beyond the power of love and forgiveness to heal?

Your notes:_____

_____

_____

_____

NINETEEN

Be sure to include a "Cast of Characters" with your autobiography. Include the relationship of each person to you as narrator. The people you and your children know will be unknown to your descendents in later generations.

See Appendix #6 for a suggestion on how to create your Cast of Characters.

#404 - HISTORICAL EVENTS

<u>Where were you</u>
- When John F. Kennedy, Robert F. Kennedy, and Martin Luther King were assassinated
- On D Day
- On December 7, 1941 (Pearl Harbor)
- On the day of the first moon landing (July 20, 1969)
- On VE and VJ Day
- On September 11, 2001 ("9/11" - the attacks on the World Trade Center and the Pentagon)
- When Secretariat won the Triple Crown
- Any date of historical significance with special meaning for you

Your notes:_____

_____

_____

_____

#405 - HEALTH

<u>What diseases, illnesses, or accidents have happened to you as you've aged?</u>
- What are your current health issues?

<u>Describe any illness, injury, or chronic conditions that changed the way you live your life</u>
- Limitations
- Unable to engage in activities due to health issues
- Changes to long and short term plans
- Fear
- Or?

Your notes:_____

_____

_____

_____

#406 - ILLNESS

<u>How do you respond to illness?</u>
- To your own illness
- To the illness of family members or friends

<u>Are you a good patient?</u>
- Do you like being cared for or would you rather be left alone?
- How well do you bear the discomfort of treatment?
- Do you do as the doctor advises, or know what's best for yourself, and act accordingly?

Your notes:_____

_____

_____

_____

#407 - CURES

<u>Have you invented any home cures for medical conditions?</u>
- Have you taught your home cures to other family members?

<u>Are there any old family cures or traditional folk medicine cures that worked for you?</u>

<u>Describe these cures</u>

Your notes:_____

_____

_____

_____

#408 - TREATMENT

If you or a loved one has ever been in long-term medical treatment, over time it can become many things: ridiculous, tragic, frustrating, frightening, and sometimes even funny.

<u>Write about a funny (or not so funny) situation when you or a loved one was in long-term medical treatment or the hospital</u>

Your notes:_____

_____

_____

_____

"Sticker"
by Ann Hamer

After two months in the hospital, after surgery and leg braces and casts and bed pans and wheel chairs and bed baths, I was finally transferred to Casita Juanita rehab hospital to begin treatment. Both arms, both legs, my right shoulder, left ankle and left collarbone were broken when I was hit by a car while out taking a walk two days after my birthday in November, 2014. By the time I went to Casita in January, I was allowed to use both arms and had 50% use of my right leg, but was still not allowed to use my left. What does 50% use even mean? How do I put 50% of my weight on one leg while not being allowed to use the other? I never quite figured it out.

A medical transport van took me to Casita on a Friday afternoon. When I arrived, the gurney on which I lay was shoved against the wall while Casita staff tried to figure out what to do with me.

"Who told her she could come?"

"How did she get here?"

"What are we supposed to do with her?"

"Is an empty room even available?"

"Where'd she come from? Maybe we can send her back."

I lay flat on my back listening to all of this while I stared at the ceiling.

"I passed Casita's admission assessment," I said. "I was told I was ready for rehab. FIND ME A ROOM!!" No way were they sending me back to Schott, the skilled nursing facility where I had lain on my back for six weeks, trussed up like King Tut's mummy.

They finally found me a room, and I was manhandled from the gurney into bed. And there I remained, abandoned and unsure of what to expect next. Hours later there was a bit of a bustle and in came a woman with a camera.

"I'm going to take pictures of your back and legs," she said. "You've been in bed a long time and we want to make sure you don't have any bedsores. Or if you do, we don't want them getting any worse."

"OK"

She rolled me over on one side and took photos of my back and hips and thighs and heels. Then she rolled me onto my other side and snapped some more pictures.

Now, when I was transferred to Casita I was still using a bed pan. Casita is a rehab hospital, and of course they wanted to transition me to using a toilet as quickly as possible. I wanted that too. But remember - no use of one leg, and only 50% use of the other leg means using a varnished slider board with a shape similar to the blade of a canoe paddle to slide from bed to wheelchair and wheelchair to toilet and then back again while trying to keep my naked behind from sticking to the board, dragging myself with my newly healed but weakened arms without touching my feet to the floor, meanwhile trying to keep the board from slipping off the toilet or the wheelchair or the bed while at the same time struggling to dislodge it from under my thighs. All while being watched by a member of Casita's staff.

You try it. Not easy. Not fun. It's scary. No wonder I got angry. Often.

Early Monday morning, an aide came in to help me get dressed and ready for my first full day in rehab. She rolled me on to my side. And started laughing. I didn't like that at all. I'm as sensitive as the next woman to having people laugh at my behind.

"Why are you laughing?" I asked.

"You have a sticker on your butt," she said.

I, ever the smart mouth, said, "What's it say - buy one get one free?"

"It says, 'left buttock,'" she said, and peeled the sticker off the aforementioned part of my anatomy.

You see, on Friday, the woman who took the photos of my backside had stuck labels on my behind for the sake of clarity in her pictures, and forgot to remove one of them.

It happens.

But honestly, how many people had looked at my behind since Friday? <u>*Lots*</u>*. Nurses, aides, doctors, therapists, pretty much anyone walking down the hall had a peek. And it didn't occur to* <u>*any*</u> <u>*one*</u> *of these people to remove the sticker?!! Did they think I labeled that part of my anatomy just in case I forgot which side was which? Hmm - - - feel around on my behind. There's the sticker. It must be my left buttock.*

But that was Casita. Wonderful rehab. Nursing care that left much to be desired. One doctor denying responsibility for a potentially fatal misstep. Another doctor finding the misstep and saving my life.

And I can walk and talk and read and write and for that I will always be <u>*very*</u> *grateful. I also lost a lot of weight. Although this is not a weight loss program I can wholeheartedly recommend, I'm grateful for that too.*

And I no longer have a sticker on my behind. And for that I am grateful as well.

#409 - DEAR GRAND

<u>Write a letter to your grandchild to be opened when she or he is 60 years old</u>

Your notes:_____

_____

_____

_____

#410 - FANTASY (2)

If you are of a certain age, you may remember the television show "Fantasy Island" and Hervé Villechaize shouting, "de plane, de plane" as the guests arrived.

<u>If you were on Fantasy Island, what would your fantasy be? Be specific about the details</u>
- What are you doing?
- Who is with you?
- What is the era of your fantasy?
- What is the location of your fantasy?

Your notes:_____

_____

_____

_____

#411 - OOPS

<u>"Why did I ever buy . . . "</u>
<u>It seemed like a good idea at the time, but it just didn't turn out the way I planned</u>
- Too expensive
- It didn't look all that good once you got it home
- You didn't use it
- It turned into another unused piece of exercise equipment
- It did not live up to your expectations

Your notes:_____

_____

_____

_____

HELPFUL HINT #50 - TAKE SOME PICTURES

Do you feel as though you've run out of ideas and don't know what to write? Take a walk around your neighborhood, using your cell phone or camera to take pictures as you wander. Print out your pictures when you get home, and use them as inspiration to start writing again.

#412 - CHANCE (1)

<u>Describe a chance meeting that changed everything</u>

Your notes:_____

_____

_____

_____

#413 - CHANCE (2)

<u>Describe a random conversation you had that changed everything</u>
- With whom were you talking?
- What was the topic of the conversation?
- What was changed?

Your notes:_____

_____

_____

_____

#414 - CINQUAIN

A cinquain is a five-line poem. In one format, the first line has one word, the second line two words, the third line three words, the fourth line four words, and the fifth line one word.

For example:

Cookies

gulped down

can give me

an extra added pound

tomorrow

They can be simple and fun or meaningful and elegant. You choose.

<u>Write a cinquain</u>

Your notes:_____

_____

_____

_____

#415 - HUMOR

<u>What is</u>
- The funniest thing you ever said?
- The funniest thing you ever heard?
- The funniest thing you ever saw?
- Your favorite joke?

Your notes:_____

_____

_____

_____

#416 - MYSTIC

<u>Describe a mystical or "other-world" experience you had</u>

Your notes:_____

_____

_____

_____

❧

Visiting a Shrine
by Ann Hamer

A few weeks ago my friend Joan came for a visit. I dug out a box where I keep some old letters and a few photos to ask her if she wanted copies of the letters she had sent me over the years. In the box were a couple of things I thought I had lost or thrown away, including an old 35mm plastic film canister with my Holy Mary Mother Virgin dirt. Here's the story.

In 1988 I was attending university in England. After Michaelmas term ended in December, I went to Turkey to visit my friend Victoria who was teaching at the American University in Istanbul. After doing the sights of Istanbul, we went to Izmir and Kushadasi on the Aegean coast. Near Kushadasi is Ephesus, and near Ephesus is the last house of the Virgin Mary. Whether or not this house is actually the last house of the Virgin Mary is unknown, since the claim is based on the visions of a

19th century nun. Nevertheless, the house has become a shrine and major Turkish tourist attraction. The house is small and ancient, and when I was there in 1988, there was nothing in the house except its dirt floor, the mud ceiling, and a raised dirt filled stone case serving as an altar. A few candles were lit in honor of Mary. If you look at pictures of the house now, there is a large altar to Mary at the entrance, and the outside walls are plastered with messages and prayers from pilgrims. None of that was there in 1988. It wasn't desolate, but it certainly was primitive.

Victoria and I were there on Christmas Eve. Since Turkey is a Muslim country, Christian holidays are not observed, but even so, there was no one there and we had the place all to ourselves. And naturally, since we were both a bit sardonic and both had highly irreverent senses of humor, we started making jokes about the house and the shrine and whether or not it really _was_ the last house of the Virgin Mary. The more we joked, the more we egged each other on, and the louder and sillier we got. I know - terrible and disrespectful - and on Christmas Eve too! So call me a heathen.

Eventually one of us - I think it was me - said, "If this is really the last house of the Virgin Mary, let's see some proof." The words had barely left my mouth when - and I swear this really happened - a chunk of the ceiling fell off and landed on the floor behind us. I admit it spooked us. We looked at each other. Nervous laughter. "Let's get out of here fast." We had been caught joking about the Virgin Mary, and like Queen Victoria, she was not amused.

Before we left, I took from my backpack an empty film canister and scooped up the dirt that had fallen from the ceiling. That is now I came to have my Holy Mary Mother Virgin dirt.

I've had it ever since. It used to be that when I opened the canister dust would spiral up - and it did that for years. Probably just because it was so dry, but who knows? I'm not going to tease or question the Virgin Mary anymore - she really doesn't like it.

I've had this canister of dirt since December 24, 1988. Over the years I've thought about throwing it out, but I just can't. So it sits in a box with other half remembered treasures - and the memory of a friend, of an amazing trip during a happy time of my life, and that visit to Mary's shrine.

#417 - STORY

<u>Write a children's story in which you are the main character</u>
<u>What character in children's literature do you most resemble?</u>
- Winnie the Pooh
- Toad of Toad Hall
- Madeline
- The Cat in the Hat
- Bambi
- One of the "Little Women"
- Nate the Great
- Tom Sawyer
- Harry Potter
- Or?

Your notes:_____

_____

_____

#418 - SEASONS

<u>How do you feel about the changing of the seasons?</u>
<u>Do you have a favorite season you anticipate more than others?</u>
- Why?

<u>Is there a season you dread more than others?</u>
- Why?

<u>Do you have more energy in one season than you do in others?</u>
<u>Do your childhood memories impact how you feel about the seasons?</u>
- School starting in the fall
- Football games and homecoming
- Summer camp

- Celebrating your birthday
- Traditional family get-togethers at certain times of the year

Your notes:_____

_____

_____

_____

#419 - FRUSTRATION

<u>What causes you to become frustrated?</u>

Your notes:_____

_____

_____

_____

#420 - RISKY

<u>Do something risky and write about it</u>
<u>What did you do?</u>
- What about this activity felt risky to you?
- What does doing something risky tell you about yourself?
<u>Does doing this risky thing give you the courage to try other risky things?</u>
- What will you do next?

Don't compare your risky behavior to the risky behavior of others. The concept of "risk" is personal to you. The idea is to push yourself out of your comfort zone, but to stay safe while doing it. Your goal is to challenge yourself and then write about it, not to spend time in an emergency room or the hospital recovering from your risk-taking.

Your notes:_____

_____

_____

_____

❧

HELPFUL HINT #51 - ORGANIZATION

Use a three ring binder to arrange your stories. By using a binder, you can try different ways of organization before you go to the expense of binding and printing your book. You can also keep adding to your stories without limit, rather than having to pay for a second volume if you rush into print too quickly.

Include with your binder clear plastic envelopes so you can add pictures to illustrate your stories. You can find plastic envelopes pre-punched with holes for three ring binders at any office supply store.

❧

#421 - I'M RIGHT

<u>Describe a time when you were right but people said you were wrong</u>

Your notes:_____

_____

_____

_____

#422 - SECRETS

<u>Describe a time you told someone else's secret</u>
- Why did you tell this person's secret?
- What was the result?

<u>Describe a time when someone told your secret</u>
- Why did this person tell your secret?
- What was the result?

<u>Describe a time when you told a secret of your own</u>
- Why did you choose to tell your secret?
- What was the result?

Your notes:_____

_____

_____

_____

#423 - SAYING GOODBYE TO OTHERS

<u>Write about the death of someone close to you</u>
- Spouse
- Parent
- Child
- Other relative
- Friend

<u>How did this person's death change your life?</u>
- What do you miss most about this person?
- How did this person's death change your relationships with other people?

<u>Reflect on the death of someone close to you</u>
- Things you wish you had said
- Things you regret you did say
- Things you wish you could ask
- Things you wish the deceased had not done to you

- Things you wish you had not done to the deceased
- A sense of relief that your loved one is no longer suffering

<u>Do you have the need to forgive this person for dying?</u>

- How do you now wish to say goodbye?

<u>Do you need to say something that wasn't said when your loved one died?</u>

Your notes:_____

_____

_____

_____

❧

"An Unwanted New Path"
by Lynda Barr

A couple of months after my twin sister Laura and I turned ten in October 1961, our world changed dramatically. My mom passed away from a brain aneurysm after being in the hospital for a week in a coma. Dad already had us staying with another family since the night Mom was rushed to the hospital. Laura and I and our younger brother Mike were taken to our mom's viewing, and I remember all the adults looking very sad, and some of the women were crying. As Laura, Mike, and I were slowly walking up to the open casket, I remember thinking that Mom was so pretty and it looked like she was just sleeping. I was beginning to have some hope that she'd be OK. A man stepped up behind us and said, "Don't worry, your mom will be back." His words began to encourage me <u>UNTIL</u> Dad flew into a rage and tried to punch the man, We heard Dad's angry words saying, "Don't you <u>ever</u> say that to my kids!!!" Some other men quickly jumped in and restrained Dad, and my next thought was that Mom was never coming back!

We continued living with friends while Dad went through the grieving process alone. It felt like we had lost him too, especially when the family we were living with moved to Oregon and we began living in stranger's homes, one after another for the next few months, until our friends in Oregon had us come live with them. Months later, Dad finally came and brought us back home. We had a series of live-in housekeeper-babysitters live with us. Finally one of them worked out, and stayed for the next couple of years. My dad slowly began dating and one of his dates, a very tall, pretty woman named Tina was quickly winning us over with her friendliness and warmth. All three of us felt very close to Tina, and hoped Dad would marry her someday. That changed one night when Tina was visiting. Another woman Dad was seeing called, and he was on the phone with her for over two hours. When Tina realized Dad was talking to another woman, she left and never came back.

A week or so later, Dad brought home Opal, the other woman. From the first moment we saw her we feared her. She sat on the couch as my dad nudged us closer to her, but we knew without a doubt she did not like us. I remember her eyes were icy cold and there was nothing but a forced smile for Dad's sake on her lips. Dad continued dating her, and every time Opal came over, she firmly showed us the correct way to cook and clean, how to dress better, and be silent and absolutely not have any say in anything. When Opal complained numerous times to Dad about us not filling the salt shaker full enough or having a small food particle on a dish after it was washed, Dad finally sat us down and said, "I don't know why you guys keep upsetting Opal, but I'm telling you right now, that no matter what, I am marrying her."

Once Dad and Opal were married, we moved into her home in El Sereno, along with Opal's three year old daughter Doreen. Laura and I were 13 and Mike was ten. From day one Opal ran the house with an iron fist, and Dad began working longer and longer hours. All he did when he got home was eat, sit down with his beer, and watch TV. He didn't want to hear our complaints and shut us out of his world. After a few months, Opal convinced Dad to send Mike off to a home for troubled boys in Colorado, where he lived until he enlisted in the Navy.

Laura and I continued to live in Opal's home, and tried to be as invisible to Opal as we could to survive her wrath each day. One time she showed us a newspaper article about a step-mom who had killed her step-kids and said "Do you see what a person can be driven to do?" I remember thinking, "You really didn't need to show us that since we are already scared to death of you!"

Once Laura and I graduated from high school in 1969 and started attending college, we ended up meeting and then marrying the first guys who paid us any attention when we were 18 years old. For Laura, it was a bus driver named Joe, and for me it was a fellow student at East LA College named Dale, who *had just gotten out of the Air Force. Laura and Joe had a son when she was 20, and Dale and I had a son when I was 20 and then a daughter when I was 22.*

❧

#424 - TAKE A CHANCE

<u>Describe a time you took a chance on someone or something</u>
<u>Describe a time when someone took a chance on you</u>
- How did it work out?

Your notes:_____

_____

_____

_____

#425 - INVENTION

<u>If you could invent something to make your own life better, what would it be?</u>
<u>If you could invent something to make the world better, what would it be?</u>

Your notes:_____

_____

_____

_____

#426 - POSTERITY

<u>What do you need to say for posterity?</u>
- I did this …

Your notes:_____

_____

_____

_____

#427 - LIMITED TIME

<u>What would you do if you had only a limited time to live?</u>

Your notes:_____

_____

_____

_____

#428 - SAYING GOODBYE YOUR WAY

<u>Write your own obituary</u>
- What do you want to say about yourself?
- What do you want people to remember about you?
- What do you hope people will **NEVER** forget about you?

<u>Plan your own funeral or memorial service</u>
- Write your own eulogy
- Write or select your own liturgy and prayers
- Select music, readings, scripture

<u>What do you want people to forget about you?</u>

Your notes:_____

_____

_____

_____

#429 - NAMING YOUR LIFE

<u>What title would you give to the story of your life?</u>
<u>In what part of the bookstore or library would your book be shelved?</u>

- Fiction and Literature
- History
- Biography and Autobiography
- Fantasy and Science Fiction
- Mystery
- Horror and Gothic
- Romance
- Cooking
- Children's Literature
- Art
- Travel

Your notes:_____

_____

_____

_____

"Just Call Me Baby"
by Maria C.

My given name is Maria Socorro. Everyone in grade school through my high school called me Socorro, but my family's nickname for me is Baby. To this day my family and close friends still call me Baby.

When we moved to Los Angeles, I used the name Maria, since it is a lot easier to spell and pronounce than Socorro. These days I am also called Mama by my five adorable grandchildren.

My aunt, Tita Abe, once told me that when I was a toddler and just starting to talk, she asked me my name. My reply was BABY NA MO (spoken in Pampango) which means JUST CALL ME BABY.

It was a simple reply from a toddler. Baby is who I am from my early years and now in my senior years. Since my book is an unpretentious recollection of my life from my toddler years to the present, why not call my book JUST CALL ME BABY. Baby is the name I love and grew up with.

My daughter Mia thinks JUST CALL ME BABY is a cute and catchy title for my book. I certainly agree, so here's my book, JUST CALL ME BABY.

#430 - EVER AFTER

<u>How do you plan to live happily ever after?</u>

Your notes:_____

_____

_____

_____

#431 - END

Some people find writing their autobiography to be both an emotional and cathartic process. You will experience great happiness as you remember past joy and success. You may also experience some sadness and feelings of regret.

This is a journey - often happy, but sometimes painful. As you write out any negativity you feel, you release yourself to tell your story with lightness, humor, and affection.

<u>What impact has writing the story of your life had on you?</u>

Your notes:_____

_____

_____

_____

APPENDICES

Appendix #1 Guidelines for Instructors

You can teach a memoir writing class using *Writing It Your Way: A Step-by-Step Guide to Telling the Story of Your Life* as your starting point, adapting the exercises to fit your available time and the needs of your class.

<u>Here are some suggestions for organizing your class:</u>

- At the first class, bring in heavy paper or card stock and colored pencils, marking pens, and crayons. Have all class members (including you) create a name plate with the name they prefer to be known by. Use the placards in every class to get to know one another.
- During the first class, distribute a hand-out with your name and contact information (phone number and e-mail address), dates, time, and place where the class will meet, and any additional rules you or the facility have, i.e. no eating in class, parking restrictions, off-limits topics, etc.
- Establish guidelines and distribute them to participants during the first class meeting.
- Create a roster with name, address, phone number, and e-mail address of each class member. Distribute the roster to all class participants at the last class.
- Bring with you to every class extra paper and pens for class members who may have forgotten theirs.
- At the first class distribute tools to help people remember their stories. The tools I distribute are the Life by Tens Tool, the Friends Tool, and the Favorites Tool which you will find in Appendix #4.

<u>Here are the guidelines Mom and distribute to our classes:</u>

- Come to class prepared to write. Bring pen, paper, computer, etc.
- We want this to be a comfortable, nonjudgmental, and safe place for you to write and share. Please respect and honor requests for privacy and confidentiality from others.
- Suggestions from class members to improve the writing of others or clarify a story point are welcome. Critical and hurtful comments are not.
- The assigned topics are meant to help you tell your story. This is not school, and you do not need to respond to all of the questions under each topic.
- Try to complete the weekly assignments to get the most out of the in-class experience.
- Every week, you will have the opportunity to read what you write to the rest of the class. You do not have to read in class if you do not want to.
- Please don't go over your allotted time when it is your turn to share.

Start a small lending library for your class with "how-to" books on writing and grammar, and biographies, memoirs and autobiographies you have enjoyed. You can find books to add to your library at used bookstores or by asking class members for books they wish to donate.

When Mom and I teach our autobiography class, we have an in-class writing exercise in which participants write for ten minutes on an assigned topic. They are also given at-home assignments to work on between class meetings. Participants are given the opportunity to read both their in-class writings and their at-home assignments to the rest of the class.

You need to accept that you can't make class members do what you want them to do, what you think is best for them, or what you think they should do. Support them in their efforts, give them lots of advice and information, and then let it go. They will create the memoir they want to create, and if they don't want to do a Cast of Characters or tell who's who in photos because people will <u>always</u> know who everyone is, so long as you have given them your advice and made the tools available, you have to accept that this is *their* choice. Don't nag. Your job is to help them tell their story in the way they want to tell it. Be at peace with yourself and your class. Anything else is too crazy-making.

APPENDIX #2 IN-CLASS WRITING EXERCISES

Mom and I learned from teaching our class that there is not enough time in the ten minutes allowed for the in-class exercises to use them to help participants remember an important event and then write about it. We now use the in-class exercises to help class members learn to loosen up and write freely. They are meant to encourage participants to think whimsically and not be constrained by writing rules or pressures to remember.

Below are some writing exercises we've used exclusively in class. You may also use some of the more esoteric exercises from this book. We have used "Drop the Reins", "Mirror", "Cake", "Shipwreck" and "On-Line" as in-class exercises.

GREETING CARDS

Your instructors have brought in a selection of greeting cards. They are in envelopes so you will not know the subject matter of the card you choose. After all class members have selected a card, open yours and begin writing.

When you open your card, something will occur to you. You may choose to write about the occasion the card honors, or the card may remind you of a special card you once received. You may not like your card, and be envious of the card chosen by another class member. It's possible nothing will come to mind, and if that happens, start your writing by describing the card.

The object of our in-class writing exercises is to help you write freely, so when you begin writing, do not censor yourself and do not over-think the exercise.

<u>Note to instructors</u> - Bring in greeting cards covering a variety of topics: birthdays, Mother's and Father's Day, holidays, thank you cards, congratulations, birth announcements, sympathy, etc. These do not need to be fancy or expensive cards. I find cards at library sales, the 99¢ Store, yard sales, and on-line.

EASTER EGGS

Yesterday was the first day of spring. Whether you celebrate Easter, Passover, or the Spring Solstice, it is a time of new beginnings. In the spirit of the season, today we will go on an Easter egg hunt.

Hidden around the room are fifteen Easter eggs. Find an egg. When you open it you will find a few treats and a number. Beginning with the lowest number, class members will select a gift bag from the selection brought in by your instructors. Unwrap the gift and begin writing.

As is the case with all of our in-class exercises, there are no right or wrong ways to approach this exercise. The idea is that you use the egg and the gift as the inspiration for your writing.

<u>Here are some suggestions:</u>
- Memories of past spring celebrations
- How you celebrate spring
- Decorating Easter eggs
- What you think about the gift you just unwrapped
- Anticipation
- Envy of someone else's surprise
- Disappointment
- Pleasure
- Amusement
- It's like getting socks and underwear for your birthday
- And?

<u>Note to instructors</u> - As with all in-class exercises, the point is to get people writing, not to distribute extravagant gifts. Keep your eyes open for inexpensive but interesting gifts to use in class.

TEN USES
10 uses for a paper clip, oven mitt, shoe, etc.

PICTURES
Select a picture or phrase from those brought in by the instructors and spend a few minutes writing about it.
- Why did you select this picture?
- What do you like about it?
- What do you dislike about it?
- Does it remind you of a happy memory or a sad memory?

Note to Instructors - These are pictures we've found in magazines and mounted on colored poster board.

ENVELOPES
Write a couple of paragraphs about your word or phrase. Please do not trade with others. Write about what you found inside your envelope.

If you can't get started, write about how you felt opening the envelope, or what the word inside looks like. Just write something.

Allow your mind to roam freely. A word may have an obvious meaning, but it may also have meanings special only to you. For example, "First love" may mean your first romantic relationship, but it may also mean the first time you saw a place you came to love, the first time you loved a car, a dog, a flower, climbing a mountain, etc.

Note to Instructors - Bring in sealed envelopes containing random words and phrases. I cut words and phrases out of magazines and advertisements. Have each class member select an envelope. Class members should open their envelopes at the same time.

ENGAGING YOUR SENSES
The details make the story.

This exercise will help you learn to engage your senses as you write. You draw in your readers and help them more fully understand your experiences if your stories describe all that you sensed. Help your reader re-live with you the taste of that first kiss, the feel and smell of your new baby, or the special scent of a holiday.

Your five senses are sight, taste, hearing, smell, and touch. Some people have a "sixth" sense - some sort of extra sensory perception.

Your instructors have brought in a selection of items designed to engage your senses. Look at them, smell them, and touch them. Listen to the sounds the items make. You are welcome to taste and eat the edible items (but not anything else!!)

Browse among the items and then return to your seat and start writing
- What memories were brought to mind by these items?
- Are you reminded of something pleasant or something you dislike?
- Use all of your senses to describe these memories so you are not only remembering, you are also re-living and inviting your readers to re-live the experience with you

If you are stuck and don't know where to start, just start writing. Describe the item using all your senses in the description, and try to let the memories come back to you as you write your description.

Remember, memories can be elusive things. Do not feel discouraged if nothing leaps immediately to mind. Right now it is important to get in the habit of writing. As with most things, the more you practice, the easier it will get.

Note to instructors - Bring in items likely to stimulate the senses and evoke memories. Some suggestions are baby powder, pumpkin pie spice, cotton, pictures cut from magazines, rough textured items, bells, soap, music boxes, peppermint, coffee, and chocolate.

Appendix #3 Guidelines for Caregivers

Your loved one[1] may be in care for a variety of reasons. You may be caring for an elderly relative. You may be caring for someone who has been diagnosed with a serious illness or a form of dementia. Each situation presents different challenges. If your older loved one is slowing down but still able to write and communicate, your role is to provide guidance, encouragement, and direction, and you may be able to work through many of the exercises in this book together. In other cases, your loved one may have a diagnosis or condition which gives you only a limited time in which to work on their autobiography.

If you and this person share a past history, try not to let _your_ memories and _your_ emotions influence or alter the memories of your loved one. Unless your loved one asks for your thoughts and memories, avoid interjecting your opinions and interpretations of past events. This is their story to tell based on _their_ memories, not yours.

Remember, illness and end of life issues are difficult and emotional for both of you, and you do not want this autobiography project to become burdensome. Find a time for your loved one to work on their autobiography, but make it enjoyable. If it becomes too much of a strain for either of you, put it aside and come back to it later.

Your loved one might resist the idea of writing an autobiography. You may hear, "My life isn't that interesting," or "I'm not a very good writer," or "No one would be interested in what I have

---

1 This guide is designed for all caregivers - both those who are paid professionals and those who care for family members or friends without compensation. Rather than refer to the person you are helping as "client / loved one", I will use the term "loved one". Caring for another person is very challenging and an act of love, even when done for compensation.

to say." Encourage your loved one, but don't lecture. Use *Writing It Your Way: A Step-by-Step Guide to Telling the Story of Your Life* and the tools provided in Appendix #4 to help your loved one tell their story.

Getting started

- Create a comfortable, nonjudgmental and safe place for your loved one to work on these exercises. Respect what is being shared by honoring requests for privacy and confidentiality. These stories belong to your loved one, and are not yours to share unless you are given permission to do so.

- The exercises are designed to help tell the story of a life. There is no need to respond to all of the questions under each topic; they are meant to help your loved one get started.

- If your loved one is facing physical or mental health issues that may limit the time available to create their autobiography, first complete the more general exercises such as growing up, school, marriage, and career, before working on the more specific topics. If your time is limited, paint with a broad brush the life story of your loved one.

- Encourage your loved one to make a regular commitment to work on their autobiography by setting goals, i.e. a certain number of pages per session or a certain number of hours per week.

- If your loved one is unable to write, try either voice recognition software for your computer, or recording the stories for transcription at a later date. Unless you are a professional stenographer, avoid taking dictation from your loved one (especially on the more detailed stories) because you are likely to miss a lot of the details - and with autobiography, the heart of the story is in the details.

- You may help your loved one remember by narrowing their focus. For example, suggest, "Tell me about your favorite elementary school teacher," rather than "Tell me about your education."

- Your loved one may have faulty memories, distort the truth, or sometimes even lie about events. This is not unusual. Insert footnotes into the finished autobiography for clarification. Do not argue with your loved one about <u>your</u> memory of what happened.

Photographs can help get your loved one started. Take out old pictures and start asking questions

- Who is in this picture?
- Where was it taken?
- When was it taken? If your loved one can't come up with an exact date or even a year, try to help them narrow down the time period. Were they in school? Do they remember where they were living at the time? Is there something about the picture that can help date it, i.e., "That was taken in Boston, and I visited Boston when I was in high school."
- What is the story of the picture? What were they doing?

Unpack the closets and open the boxes of those precious things saved by your loved one. These things were kept for a reason, and now is the time to dig them out and ask your loved one to tell their story.

Use the tools provided in the Appendices to help your loved one remember.

For the caregivers
You are entitled to feel grief and anger about the physical or mental changes in your loved one and the stress associated with care-giving. Do not be ashamed if you feel:

- Anger and sadness
- A sense of loss
- Forgotten or ignored
- Abandoned
- Loneliness
- Helplessness
- A loss of faith
- Resignation
- Acceptance

These feelings are normal. Care for yourself as you care for your loved one, and if this project gets too emotional or difficult for either of you, put it aside and return to it later.

APPENDIX #4 THE TOOLS

THE LIFE BY TENS TOOL

The Life by Tens tool is divided into ten year increments: one section for each ten years of your life. Fill out the top of each section. For example, if you were born in 1950, Section One would be 1950 - 1959 (ages 0 - 9), Section Two would be 1960 - 1969 (ages 10 - 19), and so on.

Jot down your memories for each decade. Do not try to do this chronologically; just note down one or two sentences as you remember. With these few words you will be able to select memories and stories on which you wish to elaborate. When you're stuck and don't know what to write, take a look at your Life By Tens Tool for a place to start.

Keep the Life By Tens Tool in a place where you spend a lot of time so you can jot down your thoughts as they occur to you. Memories can be elusive things, and it is important to make note of them as soon as you can, before they once again fade away.

Ages 0 through 9 (Years 19___ to 19___)

_____
_____
_____
_____
_____
_____
_____
_____
_____
_____

Ages 10 through 19 (Years 19___ to 19___)

_____
_____
_____
_____
_____
_____
_____
_____
_____
_____

Ages 20 through 29 (Years 19___ to 19___)

_____
_____
_____
_____
_____
_____
_____
_____
_____
_____

Ages 30 through 39 (Years 19___ to 19___)

_____
_____
_____
_____
_____
_____
_____
_____
_____
_____

Ages 40 through 49 (Years 19___ to 19___)

_____

_____

_____

_____

_____

_____

_____

_____

_____

_____

Ages 50 through 59 (Years _____ to _____)

_____

_____

_____

_____

_____

_____

_____

_____

_____

Ages 60 through 69 (Years _____ to _____)

_____

_____

_____

_____

_____

_____

_____

_____

Ages 70 through 79 (Years _____ to _____)

_____

_____

_____

_____

_____

_____

_____

_____

Ages 80 through 89 (Years _____ to _____)

_____

_____

_____

_____

_____

_____

_____

_____

_____

Ages 90 through 99 (Years _____ to _____)

_____

_____

_____

_____

_____

_____

_____

_____

THE FAVORITES TOOL

Listing your favorites may also help you remember.

When I was a child, my favorite actress was Haley Mills. Thinking about Haley Mills led me to thoughts about going to the movies with my family. I then remembered that when my father took us to the movies we were not allowed to get anything from the snack bar because, "We are here to watch a movie, not eat." Thinking about going to movies as a child led me to thinking about going to movies as an adult, and the discovery that my father now thought that having popcorn and a soda at the movies was a pretty good idea. Remembering one thing from my childhood resulted in a cascade of memories.

Let one memory lead to another as you think about your favorites as a child, a young adult, and now.

List your favorites

Actor_____

_____

_____

Actress_____

_____

_____

Article of clothing_____

_____

_____

Birthday dinner _____

_____

_____

Book_____

_____

_____

Building_____

_____

_____

Car_____

_____

_____

Cartoon_____

_____

_____

CD/Album_____

_____

_____

Character trait of mine_____

_____

_____

Character trait of others_____

_____

_____

Charity_____

_____

_____

Club_____

_____

_____

Collectible_____

_____

_____

Color_____

_____

_____

Cooking ingredient_____

_____

_____

Craft_____

_____

_____

Day trip_____

_____

_____

Day dream_____

_____

_____

Dessert_____

_____

_____

Drink_____

_____

_____

Elected position I held_____

_____

_____

Fantasy_____

_____

_____

Fictional character_____

_____

_____

Food_____

_____

_____

Friend_____

_____

_____

Funny person_____

_____

_____

Funny thing_____

_____

_____

Game_____

_____

_____

Grade in school_____

_____

_____

Hobby_____

_____

_____

Holiday_____

_____

_____

Holiday decoration_____

_____

_____

Hymn_____

_____

_____

Invention_____

_____

_____

Job I held_____

_____

_____

Leisure activity_____

_____

_____

Mode of transportation_____

_____

_____

Modern convenience_____

_____

_____

Movie_____

_____

_____

Music group_____

_____

_____

Part of my body_____

_____

_____

Pet_____

_____

_____

Photo of myself_____

_____

_____

Photo of others_____

_____

_____

Piece of furniture_____

_____

_____

Piece of jewelry_____

_____

_____

Place I've lived_____

_____

_____

Political leader_____

_____

_____

Possession_____

_____

_____

Prayer_____

_____

_____

Presentation I heard_____

_____

_____

Presentation I made_____

_____

_____

Recipe of mine_____

_____

_____

Recipe of someone else_____

_____

_____

Religious rite_____

_____

_____

Restaurant_____

_____

_____

Road trip_____

_____

_____

Scenic drive_____

_____

_____

Scenic view_____

_____

_____

School subject_____

_____

_____

Season of the year_____

_____

_____

Smell_____

_____

_____

Song_____

_____

_____

Sound_____

_____

_____

Sport I play_____

_____

_____

Sport I watch_____

_____

_____

Sports team_____

_____

_____

Stage play or musical_____

_____

_____

Talent I have_____

_____

_____

Talent I admire in others_____

_____

_____

Teacher_____

_____

_____

Time of day_____

_____

_____

Toy_____

_____

_____

Travel destination_____

_____

_____

TV series_____

_____

_____

TV theme song_____

_____

_____

Vacation_____

_____

_____

Vacation souvenir_____

_____

_____

Volunteer position_____

_____

_____

Wild animal_____

_____

_____

Work of art_____

_____

_____

THE FRIENDS TOOL

Listing your friends and the people you've known throughout your life is a good way to jog your memory. Although this is called "the Friends Tool", list everyone you can remember, including those people for whom you do not have fond thoughts. The people you do not like are (unfortunately!) as much a part of your life as the people you like.

<u>SAMPLE:</u>

Name: Ruth Jones

Date / Place / Circumstance: 1988 / OSU; Corvallis, Oregon / University friend

Comment: Ruth was a Canadian studying politics. She was President of the graduate students at the same time I was Treasurer. We traveled to Spain together during winter break. She returned to Canada after she took her degree. We exchanged letters for a while, but eventually lost touch. I later read in the college bulletin that she died, "suddenly, at home" in 2010.

Name: _____

Date / Place / Circumstance: _____

_____

_____

Comment: _____

_____

_____

Name: _____

Date / Place / Circumstance: _____

_____

_____

Comment: _____

_____

_____

Name: _____

Date / Place / Circumstance: _____

_____

_____

Comment: _____

_____

_____

Name: _____

Date / Place / Circumstance: _____

_____

_____

Comment: _____

_____

_____

Name: _____

Date / Place / Circumstance: _____

_____

_____

Comment: _____

_____

_____

Name: _____

Date / Place / Circumstance: _____

_____

_____

Comment: _____

_____

_____

Name: _____

Date / Place / Circumstance: _____

_____

_____

Comment: _____

_____

_____

APPENDIX #5 ORGANIZING YOUR STORY

You don't have to begin at the beginning.

Try different ways of arranging your stories, for example:
- Chronologically
- By locale, i.e. where you lived as a child, adult, in retirement
- By relationships
  - Parents and siblings
  - Other relatives
  - Spouse and children
  - Friends
  - Work colleagues
- Around collections of letters and journal entries
- By milestones and accomplishments
  - During your youth
  - During your career
  - During your retirement
- By specific events related to:
  - Play
  - Work and career
  - Military service
  - Athletics
  - School, college, or university
  - A life changing injury or illness

- ○ Vacations and travel
- ○ Marriage and children
- By your changing roles
  - ○ From dependent child to independent young adult
  - ○ From newly married to parenthood
  - ○ From parent to empty-nester
  - ○ From worker to retiree
  - ○ From child to caregiver

APPENDIX #6 SAMPLE CAST OF CHARACTERS

<u>Autobiography of Robert Charles Harper</u>

<u>Robert Charles Harper</u> ("RCH") - Born December 1, 1925 in Chicago, Illinois; died March 1, 2013 in Claremont, California

<u>Lucy Eileen Simpson Harper</u> (RCH's wife) - Born July 3, 1925 in Los Angeles, California

<u>Robert Charles Harper, Jr.</u> ("Rob") (RCH's son) - Born May 2, 1951 in Hermosa Beach, California

<u>Richard Thomas Harper</u> ("Tom") (RCH's son) - Born September 4, 1952 in Hermosa Beach, California

<u>Katherine Ann Harper</u> ("Kit") (RCH's daughter) - Born November 7, 1954 in Hermosa Beach, California

<u>Marian Collins Harper</u> (RCH's daughter-in-law; Rob's wife) - Born October 3, 1954 in Torrance, California

<u>Edward Thomas Harper</u> (RCH's grandson; Rob's son) - Born May 1, 1977 in Sacramento, California; died October 1, 1996 in Tucson, Arizona

<u>Melinda Anne Harper</u> ("Mindy") (RCH's granddaughter; Rob's daughter) - Born October 8, 1973 in Fresno, California

Charles Elroy Harper (RCH's father) - Born August 13, 1898 in Oak Park, Illinois; died June 1, 1983 in Redondo Beach, California

Millie Elizabeth Bundle Harper (RCH's mother) - Born June 29, 1894 in Grand Rapids, Michigan; died March 8, 1984 in Pasadena, California

Wilbur Robert Bundle (RCH's maternal grandfather) - Born June 15, 1866 in London, England; died _____

Sarah Hilgomitt Bundle (RCH's maternal grandmother) - Born July 4, 1869 in Guernsey County, Ohio; died _____

Mabel Bundle Schott ("Auntie Mabes") - (RCH's aunt; Millie's sister) - Born February 10, 1902 in _____ Michigan; died _____ 1986 in Detroit, Michigan

Butch Orville Schott (RCH's first cousin; Mabel's son) - born February 4, 1924 in Monroe, Michigan; died October 1, 1997 in Denver, Colorado

Include the full names of all your characters - First, middle and last names, and the maiden names of married women. Include nicknames if they are used in your stories. For example, this is the autobiography of Robert Charles Harper, who is known as "RCH". He refers to his children as Rob, Tom, and Kit, and his mother's sister as "Auntie Mabes". Be sure to include the relationship of each character to you as the narrator.

Include in your Cast of Characters all family members mentioned in your stories: spouses, children, grandchildren and great-grandchildren (biological, adopted, step and half children), parents, maternal and paternal grandparents and great-grandparents, aunts, uncles, and cousins, etc.

You can sometimes find birth and death records on the internet. If you do not have complete information, leave blanks. It is possible another family member will be able to provide the missing information.

Appendix #7 Suggested Reading

Guides for Writers

Benedetto, Mary Anne. *7 Easy Steps to Memoir Writing*

Cameron, Julie. *The Artist's Way*

Lamott, Anne. *Bird by Bird*

Roorbach, Bill. *Writing Life Stories*

San Francisco Writers' Grotto. *642 Things to Write About Me*

Stanek, Lou Willett. *Writing Your Life*

Truss, Lynne. *Eats, Shoots and Leaves*

Autobiographies and Memoirs

I recommend these books because I have read and enjoyed them all. I seldom read about politicians, military figures or media celebrities, so their stories are not on my list. I have read some of the recently published popular memoirs that "everyone" has read, but if I did not like them, they are not on my list.

I regularly search my Kindle for out-of-print books. Some of the autobiographies and memoirs I've discovered have become favorites, and are listed below. Do your own Kindle search for out-of-print memoirs and autobiographies you might enjoy.

Adamson, Joy. *Born Free*

Armstrong, Karen. *Through the Narrow Gate*

Banks, Elizabeth. *Adventures of an American Girl in Victorian London*

Bly, Nellie. *Around the World in 72 Days*

Bradlee, Ben. *A Good Life*

Brittain, Vera. *Testament of Youth*

Bryson, Bill. *The Life and Times of the Thunderbolt Kid*

Cheng, Nien. *Life and Death in Shanghai*

Corrigan, Kelly. *The Middle Place*

Day, Clarence. *Life With Father*

Devonshire, Deborah. *Wait for Me*

Gilbert, Elizabeth. *Eat, Pray, Love*

Gillard, Pierre. *Thirteen Years at the Russian Court*

Haley, Alex. *The Autobiography of Malcolm X*

Hamilton, Frederick S. *The Days Before Yesterday*

Hargrove, Marion. *See Here Private Hargrove*

Herriot, James. *All Creatures Great and Small*

Kanter, Trudi. *Some Girls, Some Hats and Hitler*

Kimmel, Haven. *A Girl Named Zippy*

Laake, Deborah. *Secret Ceremonies*

Larsen, Eric. *In the Garden of the Beasts*

Last, Nella. *Nella Last's War*

Lerner, Jimmy. *You Got Nothing Coming*

MacLean, Rory. *Stalin's Nose*

Marie Louise, Princess. *My Memories of Six Reigns*

Marshall, Catherine. *A Man Called Peter*

Mayle, Peter. *A Year in Provence*

McCourt, Frank. *Angela's Ashes*

McManus, Patrick. *The Grasshopper Trap*

Moore, Michael. *Here Comes Trouble*

Mowat, Farley. *Never Cry Wolf*

O'Hara, Kevin. *Last of the Donkey Pilgrims*

Powell, Julie. *Julie and Julia*

Remen, Rachel Naomi. *My Grandfather's Blessings*

Schaller, George. *Year of the Gorilla*
Steinbeck, John. *Travels with Charley*
Washington, Pat Beauchamp. *Fanny Goes to War*
Welty, Eudora. *One Writer's Beginnings*

Made in the USA
Columbia, SC
21 December 2017